A DERBY BOY

ANTON RIPPON

SUTTON PUBLISHING

First published in the United Kingdom in 2007 by
Sutton Publishing Limited · Phoenix Mill
Thrupp · Stroud · Gloucestershire · GL5 2BU

British Library Cataloguing in Publication Data
A catalogue record for this book is available from the British Library.

Paperback ISBN 978-0-7509-4770-1

THE AUTHOR

Anton Rippon has spent the last forty-six years (apart from three
helping to run a sports centre) in the newspaper and publishing
industry. Between 1965 and 1975 he managed the *Derby Evening
Telegraph*'s office at Burton upon Trent and later worked as a feature
writer at the newspaper's Derby office. As a freelance his work has
appeared in national newspapers including *The Times, Independent,
Guardian* and *Sunday Telegraph*, and many national magazines. Anton
has written documentary series for BBC Radio Derby and appeared on
national radio and regional television. He also wrote and co-produced
the highly acclaimed documentary film *The Derby County Story*. He has
had over twenty books published, mostly on sport but also on the
history of his home town of Derby. Today he writes a popular weekly
column in the *Derby Evening Telegraph*. For over twenty years he ran
Breedon Publishing, the company he co-founded in 1982 and which
he sold in 2003 to resume writing. Married to Pat, he lives in
Mickleover. Their daughter, Nicola, is herself a freelance writer with
several books to her name.

Typeset in 11/12pt Plantin.
Typesetting and origination by
Sutton Publishing Limited.
Printed and bound in England.

Contents

Introduction

The first stirrings of this book came all of seventeen years ago, and in the unlikeliest of settings: a plush restaurant over Grand Central Station, high above Manhattan. I was there to lunch with a man called Clive Toye, a former Fleet Street journalist who had gone to the USA in the early 1970s to be in at the beginnings of the North American Soccer League. Clive eventually became general manager, and then president, of the world-famous New York Cosmos team. Now he was looking forward to the World Cup being staged in the States in 1994 and, with four years still to run, he was exploring various business opportunities. That was where I came in. At the time I owned a publishing company; Clive wanted to take our book on the World Cup and republish it on his side of the Atlantic. Business over, and coffee served, we began to talk of our own British origins. I remarked that, when I'd started grammar school in Derby, in 1956, places like America seemed inaccessible to a working-class boy like me. You might as well have told me that, one day, I would fly to the Moon as tell me that I'd eventually get to New York. By 1990, the United States was a country that I'd visited many times, but still I could never quite get over the wonder of it all. Even at that moment, as I looked down at the busy intersection of 42nd Street and Lexington Avenue, I marvelled at the fact that here I was, a lad from Gerard Street, sitting in New York talking to the man who signed Pele for the Cosmos. Then Clive said, 'You know, you should write a book about it . . . about what it was like to grow up in a place like Derby after the war.' When I got back to my hotel that evening – and with nothing much on the television – I began to make some notes. Then I put them away, returned to England the next morning, and left it at that. For the next few years I was too busy publishing other people's books to write one myself.

In 2003 I sold the business and found myself a freelance writer once again, able to wander, in a literary sense at least, wherever I wanted. More easily managed working hours also meant that, with John Burns and Colin Shaw, boyhood pals from Gerard Street, I could relive parts of my childhood through long, lazy days revisiting old haunts: a sort of *Last of the Summer Wine* but without the scenery (we had firm ideas about who was cast as Compo, Clegg and Foggy). More often than not, however, I would make these journeys on my own. Every time I was in the vicinity I would be drawn back to the area where I'd grown up and which had shaped the person I became. In the summer of 2006 I went to visit a former neighbour, Jessie Manning, who lived in Webster Street, a few yards from our old back gate. It was a scorching summer's day and I spent the afternoon in the cool of her living room, drinking tea, munching cakes, and taking the usual stroll down memory lane. Now it was time to leave. As I wandered back down Gerard Street, it occurred to me that now might be a good time to dust off that notebook and resurrect Clive Toye's suggestion. So here we are.

What follows is my account of growing up in the East Midlands industrial town (as it then was) of Derby, from the end of the Second World War until 1975, by which time I'd married and become a father. The characters mentioned in the following pages are all real people and I've changed no names, although I haven't dwelt on incidents that might unduly embarrass others. There is also the indulgence of a little family history in an attempt to describe Derby in the 100 or so years before I was born. The book ends in the middle of the 1970s simply because the second half of that decade heralded a significantly different sort of Derby; the purpose of telling my story was to attempt a picture of town life in an era that would be unfamiliar to anyone born later. The mid-1970s also saw my own life change. Working at Derby Sports Centre brought its own dramas before I returned to newspapers. There followed a spell as a feature writer back on the staff of the *Derby Evening Telegraph*, and a short stint in the features department of the *Nottingham Evening Post*, before the freelance life beckoned. There were happy years spent covering football for the *Sunday Telegraph*, and writing documentaries for BBC Radio Derby, all of which brought me into contact with many boyhood heroes, some of whom became good friends. Radio appearances on such varied shows as Pete Murray's on Radio Two and Tommy Vance's on British Forces Network also provided interesting diversions. There were also some books, mostly on sport but occasionally on the history of Derby; running a business can be hugely rewarding, but there is nothing to compare with the prospect of a day with nothing to do but write. Writing also presents the opportunity to dip in and out of other people's lives. Now I am dipping back into my own.

There are a number of people to thank: Clive Toye, obviously, for suggesting that my memories might be worth recording; my agent, John Pawsey, for agreeing and for his advice which, as always, was priceless (but don't tell him that); and Simon Fletcher at Sutton Publishing for also seeing merit in the idea. As always, my friend and occasional co-author, Andrew Ward, was full of encouragement; his filing system is also better than mine because he'd recorded stories that I'd told him years ago and then forgotten. *Salaam Stanley Matthews*, the autobiography of Poupee Gupta, a contemporary of mine at grammar school in Derby, provided inspiration on days when I was flagging. Other former schoolmates helped in diverse ways: Ken Walker encouraged me at every step; John Cheadle just took the mickey and kept my feet on the ground. My old pal, Ron Frost, entertained me with memories of his own early working life; I wish I had room to include them here. Jill Dean at the *Derby Evening Telegraph* was a great help with photographs.

Pat and Nicola, meanwhile, must hope that, now half a lifetime's anecdotes have finally been committed to print, they will never have to listen to them again. But I wouldn't put money on it.

Anton Rippon, Derby

CHAPTER ONE

Roll Out the Barrel

It was the last winter of the Second World War. Field Marshal Gerd von Rundstedt was making a desperate attempt to break through Allied lines in the Ardennes, American band leader Glenn Miller was missing over the English Channel, Norway was suffering an acute shortage of herring oil, and my heavily pregnant mother decided to come home from the butcher's in Abbey Street on the back of a neighbour's ancient motor-bike. Later that foggy Wednesday evening – 20 December 1944 – I was born in a front bedroom of our terrace house in Gerard Street, half a mile from Derby's town centre. I hadn't been due until the New Year but, the previous evening, my mother had fallen over a milk churn in the blackout. That, and being bounced around on a motor bike, apparently hastened my appearance. Everyone was surprised that I wasn't a girl; there was a local saying that Abbey Street was so badly maintained by the council that it would have shaken the balls off anybody. What happened next has been only partially documented: von Rundstedt failed in his bid to change the course of the war; they never did find Glenn Miller; the Norwegians sorted out their herring oil problem; and I grew up in grey, austere postwar Derby.

Actually, 20 December was already an exciting day in the town, even before I made my unscheduled appearance. A few hundred yards from where I was born, six escaped German prisoners-of-war were being recaptured by two policemen and a Corporation bus driver outside the offices of the Derby Gas, Light and Coke Company in Friar Gate. The Germans had escaped from a POW camp in Staffordshire but their luck ran out, their stolen car breaking down opposite Derby's Full Street police station. After a short chase through the town centre, they were rounded up, the last one collared by a bus driver on his way to start the early shift. As the bedraggled and thoroughly miserable Germans began their melancholy journey back to prison camp, my mother, unaware that the Wehrmacht had been just down the road, laboured away in a front bedroom with the assistance of the family physician, Dr Latham Brown, who, when he wasn't introducing new Derbeians to the world, doubled up as the local police surgeon. My father sat downstairs fiddling with the wireless set, switching between *The Bob Hope Programme* on the General Forces station and *Paul Adams and his Mayfair Music* on the Midland Home Service. Eventually, getting on for midnight, I appeared, just in time for Christmas. I've always liked a party and obviously didn't want to miss this one, even if it was to be blunted by blackout regulations, food rationing and the occasional marauding German looking for a spare part. My mother chose to name me after Anton Walbrook, the Viennese-born actor who'd just starred in the film *Dangerous Moonlight*. Considering that we were at war with the Hun, my father roundly disapproved of such a Germanic name, so much so that when he was despatched to register my birth ten days later, my mother wasn't sure whether he would follow her wishes. She was relieved when she saw my birth certificate. I expect he just thought, 'Anything for a quiet life.' Whatever his reasoning, he spent the first ten years of my life calling me 'Tich', and then, until the day he died, by which time I was thirty-seven, 'Mate'. I don't remember him ever calling me 'Anton'.

Although I was blissfully unaware of it, Derby was enduring an average sort of war. Years later, I read the statistics: 148 air-raid alerts; 45 civilian deaths due to enemy action; 152 high-explosive bombs; 164 incendiary bombs. Tragic though this was, compared to many British industrial towns and cities it was small beer. Indeed, a measure of how safe Derby could be considered in comparison to other places can be drawn from the fact that my parents had actually fled back to the town during the war. In 1937 my father, who was a newspaper linotype operator, had taken a job on the *Hull Daily Mail*. Two years later, on that historic Sunday morning of 3 September 1939, he and my mother were huddled round a wireless set in the front room of their house in Aisne Street, Hull, listening to Prime Minister Neville Chamberlain announce that ' . . . consequently,

this country is at war with Germany'. According to my mother, my father sent her straight down to Hull Labour Exchange first thing on the Monday morning to register him in a reserved occupation so that he wouldn't have to do military service. Not that either of them failed to see their fair share of danger. For the next two years, nights in the Rippons' air-raid shelter were followed by tentative explorations to see what further damage had been wreaked by the Luftwaffe on what was to become one of the most heavily bombed British cities of the Second World War. As the centre of Hull was steadily being demolished by Goering's air force, each morning my father picked his way through the previous night's rubble to get to work wearing a

Alec and Phyllis Rippon pictured shortly before they left Derby for Hull in 1937. (Author's Collection)

The scene that greeted my father when he went to work in the centre of Hull after a German air-raid in May 1941. A few days later, my parents decided to move back to Derby. (Hull Daily Mail)

Hull Daily Mail armband so that the police would let him through cordoned-off streets. Each teatime he would return with the news: 'The docks copped it again last night' or 'There aren't any houses left in Grindell Street.' Parts of Jameson Street, where the *Mail* offices were situated, were badly damaged. Often he went straight down to work after a hair-raising night spent fire-watching on the roof of the *Mail* building.

The house in Ainse Street backed on to allotments and, long before the nightly warning siren wailed out, my parents knew that another raid was imminent because of the frantic activity around the anti-aircraft gun that was sited just over their garden fence. One night, tired of huddling in the shelter, they remained in the house. At the height of the raid, my mother got bored and stuck her head out of the back door to see what was going on. Suddenly there was a high-pitched whooshing noise and my father grabbed her by the hair and pulled her back in. I still have the large chunks of shrapnel that missed her by a few inches. Things got worse. A young girl was blown into their garden after a bomb fell nearby; the girl survived but her parents, neighbours of my mother and father, were killed. Down the street, three Scottish soldiers died when a blast bomb fell nearby, stripping them naked but leaving their bodies unmarked. Out doing the shopping one morning after a raid, my mother and a neighbour were stopped by an ARP warden who told them that a human ear had just been found in the road. More than 1,200 citizens of Hull were killed and 95 per cent of the city's houses damaged in some way or other. When the houses directly opposite my parents' home were flattened (the blast throwing my mother from one end of their hallway to the other), it was the final straw; they decided it was time to return to Derby. It was May 1941 and, had it not been for the war, they would have remained in Hull. So I have Adolf Hitler to thank for the fact that I wasn't born a Yorkshireman. We have a saying in Derbyshire: you can always tell a Yorkshireman, but you can't tell him much.

Back in Derby, my parents lodged at 147 Abbey Street before, in October that year, renting from the landlord of the Bell and Castle on Burton Road, a large end-of-terrace house on the corner of Webster Street and Gerard Street, not far from where my mother had grown up in Abbey Street. The *Derby Evening Telegraph* had no vacancies – a wartime shortage of newsprint meant that most newspapers were reduced to perhaps four or eight pages (and few businesses could afford to advertise anyway) – but my father had managed to get a job on the weekly *Long Eaton Advertiser*, which meant a tedious daily journey on a Barton's bus that had its windows painted blue and its internal lights a dull amber to help maintain the blackout. He would set off at about six in the morning and sometimes didn't return home until after ten at night, a routine that I remember well because it continued until he could get back on the *Telegraph* in the summer of 1956.

It didn't suffer as badly as Hull, but Derby was also bombed. This is Offerton Avenue, Normanton, after the town's heaviest air-raid of the war, in January 1941. (Derby Evening Telegraph)

Life began to settle down again, the main improvement being that, compared with Hull, air-raids were few and far between and it was possible to get a good night's sleep once more. My mother renewed pre-war Derby friendships, particularly with Stan and Dolly Gregory, a Sheffield couple who ran a fish and chip shop in Abbey Street. She joined the long queues that formed outside Derby's shops, often without knowing what was actually on sale that day, and generally tried to carry on as normal until she received a rude awakening. One day, a man from the Ministry of Labour and National Service knocked on the door of the house in Gerard Street. My mother was still in her early thirties; she had to report for war work in one of the many Derby factories that had been turned over to producing munitions. This was a major shock because she hadn't worked since 1935, when she'd left Dould's mill in Spa Lane, to get married. There was an alternative, however: she could provide billets for servicemen instead, an option to which she quickly signed up. The men were from the Royal Signals and were stationed at the telephone exchange in nearby Colyear Street. One of them stood 6ft 8in tall and was universally known as Nelson, after the column, I suppose. Another, a Russian, was some kind of electronics genius. He was also an accomplished musician who spent his off-duty hours playing classical music on the family piano, to the delight of my parents and his army colleagues alike. Until, that is, he made a dramatic exit. One hot summer's afternoon, two military policeman hammered on the front door, looking for the Russian. Seconds later, he leapt out of the open front-room window and fled down Gerard Street, the redcaps in pursuit. My parents never saw him again and never learned of his fate, although my mother soon discovered that, as he made his escape, the mysterious Russian had grabbed a row of pearls given to her by her cousin Fred, who, before the war, had been a rubber planter in Malaya.

'Oh well,' she said later, 'I suppose he was desperate.' She hadn't a clue what he'd done to attract the attention of the authorities, and she didn't really care. She always had a soft spot for a rebel and the Russian's role in bringing a little colour into an otherwise drab and difficult world was more than sufficient compensation. For years after the war we had his business card, printed in the Cyrillic alphabet. Sadly, through several house moves, I lost it long before becoming interested enough in his story to research it further. I still do have, however, a pre-war Russian banknote that he left behind. Perhaps it was some kind of payment for the pearls after all.

By the time I was born, the war had taken a dramatic turn in the Allies' favour. By the spring of 1944 the people of Derby realised that an Allied invasion of the European mainland couldn't be far off. National Fire Service personnel, barrage balloons and heavy anti-aircraft batteries left the town to defend the Channel ports where there was a massive build-up of Allied troops. The defence of Derby was left in the hands of the local Home Guard units and their 'Z' rocket batteries. Road and rail traffic southwards increased and the canvas covers couldn't disguise the tell-tale shapes of landing craft. Column after column of tanks and armoured cars snaked their way around the relatively new Derby ring road, heading south; overhead, Dakotas towed gliders through the skies. The military camps around Derby became deserted as the huge invasion army was assembled on the south coast. One night in April, everyone in the neighbourhood thought that the invasion had begun when a large air convoy created an impressive spectacle as the green and red navigation lights of both gliders and transport planes made a brilliant pattern in Derby's night sky. That was a false alarm but, as invasion day grew ever nearer, the significance of this truly awesome adventure came home fully to the neighbours working long shifts to produce munitions in Derby's factories, or simply gossiping in the pub – when beer was available – or the corner shop. As June 1944 came, they went to bed each night with a sense of great events impending. They knew that any day now would come news of the battle that would alter the course of their lives, and the lives of their children (I was now well on the way), for ever. On the morning of 6 June 1944, the newspapers and early morning radio news were full of the fall of Rome, which had been announced the day before. But just after 9 a.m. came the brief announcement: 'Under the command of General Eisenhower, Allied naval forces supported by strong air forces began landing Allied armies this morning on the coast of France.'

Hardly had the Normandy beachheads been established when Derby began to see something of the other side of the picture. On 13 June, only a week after D-Day, the first convoy of wounded soldiers arrived at the Midland station. Waiting to meet a friend from Hull who was coming down for a few days' visit, my pregnant mother watched a grim procession of stretchers carrying casualties from trains to the waiting ambulances. Men in hospital blue became a familiar sight in Derby. Before long, the effects of the Germans' campaign of 'flying-bombs' – the V1s and later V2s which terrorised southern cities – began to be felt. Even though Derby was beyond the range of these latest weapons of destruction, the first 'doodlebug' evacuees began to arrive, first in a trickle and then in a flood as the official scheme was made fully operative. Between July and September, when the rocket sites in northern Holland were captured by the Allies, Derby received 8,000 evacuees. There was no question of any coming to live at our house in Gerard Street; it was still full of soldiers. December 1944 saw the Home Guard, including the lovely man who would one day become my father-in-law, lay down their arms. They had never been called into action, but they would have been ready to defend the town against German invaders had the call come. Two days before Christmas, Derby Corporation bus crews (when they weren't recapturing escaped POWs) went on strike in a dispute over new timetables. Rumours of the action had spread and most shoppers had gone home at lunchtime, thus avoiding the disruption. Of course, I hardly needed a bus. I was only three days old. For my mother, there was always the back of that neighbour's motor-bike.

A few weeks after I was born, Nelson and his fellow signallers took leave of our house. Nelson kept in touch, returning to visit a few times after the war. I have the faintest recollection of this giant in khaki, so I assume he must have remained in the services. Before he left Gerard Street, however, Nelson had one more duty to perform. A couple of weeks into January 1945, I was baptised at St Werburgh's Church on the corner of Cheapside and Friar Gate, a few yards from where the German POWs had been recaptured three weeks earlier. Nelson was there, acting as a proxy godfather for Uncle Jack, my father's brother and a Desert Rat who had fought with the Eighth Army at El Alamein. Uncle Jack was by now serving in Palestine; for some reason, the Army wouldn't let him come back just for one day. My godmother was a lady called Sylvia, who ran a grocer's shop at the corner of Gerard Street and Grey Street. I am unsure as to the exact duties of godparents, but my only recollection of Sylvia is of her husband bribing me with a penny to say 'bugger'. That apart, she seems to have had no real impact on my life. Indeed, although St Werburgh's was the oldest site of continuous Christian worship in Derby, my early introduction to such a venerable religious venue had no profound effect upon me either. It was 1953 before I made my second appearance there, for my grandmother's funeral. Then a grammar school carol concert in 1956, and that was it. St Werburgh's was made redundant in the 1980s and then had a brief spell as a shopping arcade. At the time of writing there are plans to turn it into a restaurant. Unlike 1945, hardly anyone goes to church these days.

In March 1945, the first consignment of lemons to be seen in the town for three years arrived in Derby. For my parents it was one of those small but significant events which signalled that a return to pre-war normality might not be far away. Alas, the early postwar years were going to prove anything but normal. Food rationing actually became more severe, which led to my mother making a huge compromise with her morals. Despite being scrupulously honest almost to the point of eccentricity, there was one area where she soon became happy to dabble on the wrong side of the law: the Black Market. Down our street, in a house on the other side of Wilson Street, lived a busy little woman whom I knew only as Mrs Potter. She could often be seen scurrying about the neighbourhood after dark, lugging a huge sack on her back. For several years after the war, Mrs Potter still operated in this manner. One day, I answered the door to her furtive knock, to be told in an anxious whisper, 'Go and see if your mother wants any tea.' Naturally my mother did want some tea – or sugar, or butter, or anything else that was on ration – and money and consumables changed hands on the darkened front step. The goods had been stolen, of course, but even otherwise law-abiding housewives desperately wanted to put a little extra on their families' tables.

But if my first Christmas had been hampered by wartime rationing (probably not as there was obviously no government restriction on mother's milk), there was another, bigger, party the following May. I lay in my mother's arms as she stood on the doorstep watching the neighbours celebrate VE night, although the significance of grown-ups performing the conga along Gerard Street while singing 'Roll Out the Barrel' naturally passed by a five-month-old baby. That August, victory over Japan left me similarly mystified, as did yet another celebration: in April 1946, when I was sixteen months old, my mother perched me on the wall of St Peter's Church to watch Derby County parade the FA Cup through the town on an Offiler's beer dray. I like to think that I remember

August 1945: VJ Day celebrations in Derby Market Place. Like the VE Day celebrations three months earlier, their significance went over my infant head. (Derby Evening Telegraph)

Derby County parade the FA Cup through the town in spring 1946. I was in the crowd, although I don't remember. None of the players remembered me either. (Derby Evening Telegraph)

Cousin Sid Rippon and his bride, seventeen-year-old Nancy Weir, at their wedding in Auckland, New Zealand. A few weeks later Sid sailed for North Africa. He died in an Italian POW camp. Nancy never remarried. (Author's Collection)

it, but I probably got the images from photographs that I saw later. Certainly, when I interviewed the eight surviving members of that famous team for a radio series in 1984, none of them remembered seeing me. I've always been grateful to my mother for taking me with her that late spring day. Both she and my father had a sense of history and whenever anyone talks about the day the Rams paraded the trophy through Derby for the only time in their history, at least I can say, 'I was there!'

Like most families, ours had been touched by wartime tragedy. In November 1941, my Uncle Eric (a pre-war dance band star under the name of Barrie Gray and brother of Derby's world-famous crooner Denny Dennis) had been lost in the North Atlantic after his merchant ship, SS *Stonepool*, was torpedoed by a U-boat. Eric had married my mother's sister, Esther, in 1933, while he was working as a musician at the King's Café in Derby. Then, in October 1942, my father's cousin, Sidney Rippon, had died in an Italian prisoner-of-war camp after being captured while serving with New Zealand forces in North Africa. Only a few weeks before he was posted overseas, Sidney had met and married Nancy Weir, a beautiful seventeen-year-old girl from Auckland. After he sailed for the war, Nancy never saw him again, but she never remarried. 'He was the only man I ever loved', she said.

Ready for the toils and efforts that lay ahead? As Britain prepared for her first postwar winter, I had my photograph taken on a neighbour's kitchen table. (Author's Collection)

In November 1945, Grandma Rippon sent me a birthday card from her home in the Lincolnshire fenland town of Spalding. Whether she was pre-empting a delay in the postal service, or whether she just got the date wrong, I don't know, but I still have the card. Actually, it isn't a birthday card in the traditional sense, simply a postcard showing a cartoon of a small boy and his dog, and a quote from Winston Churchill upon announcing to Parliament, six months earlier, the German surrender: 'Let us not forget the toils and efforts that lie ahead.' It isn't the sort of sentiment you would normally send anyone on their birthday, let alone a one-year-old. But then again, life in postwar Britain was going to be tough. Why wrap it up?

CHAPTER TWO
Our Mixed-up Family

In 1953, my maternal grandmother, who had lived with us in Gerard Street, died a sad death in Derby's Kingsway mental hospital. She'd been increasingly ill for some time before. The previous November, she'd got out of bed in the middle of the night and pulled a wardrobe on top of her, cutting her head. She was patched up and, in the morning, the family doctor was summoned. There was nothing else for it: he committed her to the mental hospital. She wasn't mad; she was just old. Today, they have names for conditions like hers; fifty years ago they just gave it the undignified label of 'senile decay'. An ambulance called to collect her and I never saw her again. Four months later, on the afternoon of Friday 13 March, in Coronation Year, I'd just got home from school when there was a knock on the front door. A man asked to speak to my mother. He handed her a note from the hospital. Gran Rowley had died in Kingsway that afternoon. She was eighty-four. My mother's first reaction was to draw all the curtains; in those days it was the first thing anyone did when there was a death in the family. On the eve of her funeral, Gran was brought home one more time. My mother said she would have been appalled at the idea of simply being driven up to the front door and away again. The following day, after a service at St Werburgh's, she was buried at Nottingham Road cemetery. I tossed a small bunch of violets into her grave. I was eight years old.

Only in the days following her funeral did I learn that the gentle Victorian lady with the soft London accent and the big blue veins on her hands, the lady who played 'Home Sweet Home' on our piano and who loved to listen to the Saturday evening dance music radio programme *Take Your Partners*, the lady whose failing eyesight I'd continually tested by imploring, 'Just one more story please, Gran,' the lady who I'd always believed was my mother's mother, was actually her aunt who had adopted her. Therefore, Jane Eliza Rowley was really my great-aunt, which meant that my mother was her own cousin and I was my own second cousin. Suddenly I had a grandfather who lived only a few streets away, which came as a surprise since I'd always thought that my grandfather on that side of the family had died in 1921. And so he had, but now it turned out that that man was also my great-uncle. Such was the complicated – and sometimes tragic – story that ran through my mother's side of our family. Their tale also spans a hugely significant period in Derby's history.

Some time during the mid-1820s, my great-great-great-grandparents arrived in what was then a bustling market town. They'd been heading this

A fine Victorian couple: William and Jane Rowley, who were both my adopted grandparents and my great-uncle and aunt. (Author's Collection)

way for some time. George Rowley was born at Blithfield, in Staffordshire, in 1779. He and his wife, Sarah, had seven children, each one born at different points on a twelve-year journey which saw the family move from Abbot's Bromley, to Yoxall, Maer, Shardlow, Aston-on-Trent and Mackworth where the last child, Francis, was baptised in 1822. They arrived in Derby – the open Markeaton Brook was still flowing right through the middle of the town – to take over the Stag and Pheasant public house at 29 Lower Brook Street on the edge of what was to become Derby's infamous West End. George and Sarah found a town that was still very much geared to the agricultural area in which it lay, the heavy industry which was to make Derby's name famous throughout the world still some years away. As the Rowleys moved in, even the Crown Derby china works in nearby King Street was still recovering from a period of recession. George and Sarah would have found a skyline that featured few factory stacks, most prominent among them that of the 150ft-high Shot Tower in the Morledge, where molten lead was poured through sieves at the top of the tower to be formed into tiny droplets as they spun through the air. The Silk Mill, claiming to be England's first proper factory, would also have caught their eye, for Derby's main industry then seems to have been textile manufacturing. Most of all, though, the Rowleys' little pub was dominated by the newly opened Rykneld Mills, a steam-powered textile mill that towered over nearby Bridge Street.

George and Sarah Rowley were to witness many events in Derby's history: the building of a new Guildhall; the town's main public buildings being lit by gaslight for the first time; the new county gaol opening in Vernon Street, which was good for their trade; and the Reform Bill Riots when a mob rampaged just up the road in Friar Gate, the Derby militia was called out, shots were fired and three men lost their lives. That would probably have been a good night to put up the shutters at the Stag and Pheasant. No doubt they would also have served strikers who took part in the Derby Lock Out, one of the most famous chapters in the history of the trades union movement when workers all across the town joined those who had walked out when a silk mill owner dismissed one of their colleagues who'd refused to accept a fine for alleged shoddy workmanship. Again there was violence but, late in 1834, a Bill was passed through Parliament confirming the rights of workers to form trades unions, and the Derby Lock Out entered the annals of union folklore. Whether George and Sarah were sympathisers, I have no way of knowing. I imagine that they weren't too bothered one way or the other, so long as the takings held up at the Stag and Pheasant.

Two years later, in 1836, George died at the age of fifty-seven. He was buried in the churchyard at St Werburgh's. Sarah continued to run the pub on her own for a number of years, by which time she'd been joined in the licensed trade by one of her sons, William, who, with his wife, Alice Swanwick, had taken over the Rising Sun in Friar Gate, opposite

The Rising Sun in Friar Gate, where my great-great-grandfather was landlord in the 1840s. (Derby Museum & Art Gallery)

St Werburgh's. The Rising Sun was one of the oldest sites of a licensed house in Derby. The low brick-clad timber-framed building with a thatched roof was a far cry from the pub of the same name which was rebuilt in 1888 and which is today called the Bishop Blaize. William and Alice lived in a different sort of Derby to the one that George and Sarah had first set eyes on twenty years earlier. The railway had arrived in the town in 1839, pulling up at a temporary wooden platform; Derby's first purpose-built station, at Castlefields, was now open for business. In the Litchurch area, Derby Arboretum, the first urban public park in England, had also opened its gates for the first time, giving the likes of William and Alice Rowley the opportunity to view the 1,000 trees and thousands more bushes and shrubs planted there. Sunday was probably the only day they could visit the park, but since that was the one day on which there was free admission it probably suited them. With its new railway and ever-growing number of factories, Derby was becoming an industrial centre to rival any in Britain. But the greatest change that William and Alice would have noted would have been the development of the town centre where Markeaton Brook was culverted, its bridges disappearing in the process, and Brookside was now named Victoria Street after the new young queen. The Athenaeum Society then oversaw a development on the corner of the Cornmarket and Victoria Street, where a bank, post office and the Royal Hotel sprang up, half a mile down the road from the Rising Sun. And if the new Guildhall in the Market Place burned down in 1841, not to worry because a new one arose on the same site soon afterwards, using much of the old shell.

The development of Derby's town centre would have been good for business at the Rising Sun, but the best days must surely have been reserved for the public executions which took place just up the road, outside the county gaol in Vernon Street. On public hanging days, Derby's pubs enjoyed their best takings of the year and the Rising Sun would have enjoyed a prime location as thousands of people flocked up Friar Gate. Street traders, musicians, entertainers, food hawkers – and pickpockets – all lined the route taken by crowds sometimes numbering between 20,000 and 40,000, many of whom had arrived on special trains. Occasionally there were mass fights and it was probably as much on the grounds of safety as for any moral issues that the grisly spectacle of public hangings was eventually banned. The last one in Derby was in 1862, after a jealous lover called Richard Thorley used a razor to cut the throat of a young woman called Eliza Morrow at her home in Agard Street, on the other side of Friar Gate. Around 20,000 attended Thorley's execution and quite a few of them would have crowded into the Rising Sun. By then, however, William and Alice had left the pub and moved up the road to 72 Ashbourne Road from where William worked as a 'gentleman's gardener'. Seven years later he died, like his father at the age of fifty-seven.

His five children were all still living in Derby, although none had followed in the family tradition of the licensed trade. One of them, however, my great-grandfather William Rowley, although a cabinet maker and machine joiner by trade, did eventually marry into the pub business.

Derby's county prison in Vernon Street. Public hangings took place here, which was good for business so far as my inn-keeping forebears were concerned. They ran a pub just round the corner. (Author's Collection)

William's first wife, my great-grandmother Eliza Hough, who was a distant cousin of the world-famous potter Thomas Whieldon, had endured a hard life even by the standards of nineteenth-century working-class Britain. By the time she died, at the tragically young age of thirty, Eliza had borne six children and raised them and two of her siblings after both her parents had themselves died at a relatively young age. Eliza died at the family home at 27 Markeaton Street in March 1873, from complications following the birth of a son, John. Two years later, William, now left with a young family to raise, was married to Ann Taylor, the widowed landlady of the Old White Horse, another of Friar Gate's timber-framed thatched hostelries that stood at right-angles to the road. Soon after their marriage, the pub was controversially demolished, to make way for yet another railway station – Friargate, run by the Great Northern Railway on the Nottingham–Chesterfield line – and when Ann was not permitted to transfer the licence to other premises in the town, it meant that William the younger lost his chance to follow in his father's footsteps. William and Ann had four children. Meanwhile, his six children by the tragic Eliza were beginning to make their own way in the world.

My grandfather, Frank – the man who, for the first eight years of my life, I didn't know existed – left school in 1882 to become a junior footman at the Royal Hotel where he lived in. He, too, became a pub landlord, running a beer house called the Derby Volunteer in Hope Street, near Derby's first railway station. One of his brothers, Frederic, a solicitor's clerk, lived at 12 Campion Street, one of the streets climbing

My natural grandfather, Frank Rowley, was a junior footman at the Royal Hotel in Victoria Street (below).
He met my grandmother, Sarah Craig, when visiting his brother. (Author's Collection/W.W. Winter)

away behind Ashbourne Road. Next door to Frederic – who, in August 1897, was to die from typhoid fever meningitis – lived the Craig family. George Craig was a traveller in skins and hides, and his children were born all over the place, even Belgium (by a cruel twist of fate, my great-uncle, Alexander Craig, was to die in Flanders only a mile or so from where he was born, killed while serving with the Sherwood Foresters at Poperinge in September 1915). One daughter, Sarah, had first seen the light of day in the less than salubrious surroundings of Water Street, Bootle. On his regular visits to his brother, Frank was soon attracted to her. They married at Derby Register Office in June 1898. Four daughters were born: Doris in February 1899, May in the summer of 1906, Esther in March 1909 and, finally, my mother, Phyllis, on 20 October 1912, at the family home which was now 251 Nottingham Road, llkeston. Eight days later, Sarah died following complications at the birth. Frank's career as a publican had failed and he was now a poorly paid horse driver at Stanton Ironworks. As he already had three children to support, my mother was adopted by Frank's brother, William Rowley, and his wife, Jane, the lady we met at the beginning of this chapter. My mother was unaware of this until she was seven years old, when a neighbour whom she'd annoyed told her out of spite; the death of her mother in childbirth was something which affected her for the rest of her life.

I was almost fifty before I knew the name of my natural maternal grandmother, whereupon I set out to track down Sarah Rowley's grave. The trail took me to Park Cemetery at Ilkeston, one cold, grey November afternoon in 1994. The attendant led me past gravestone after gravestone before marching on to a patch of grass and unceremoniously stabbing the ground with a flower cane. 'About here', he said, before leaving me to it. I was expecting a headstone; of course, in the dire circumstances in which the family found themselves in 1912, there had been no money for such a luxury.

William and Jane Rowley lived with their adopted daughter at their tobacconist's shop at 167 Abbey Street, from where William also ran an insurance round. It was a happy life. One of my mother's fondest memories was of her adopted father (only she never ever used the word 'adopted') meeting her from Gerard Street School, her hair tied in a mass of pink ribbon. She recalled how she slipped her hand into his and skipped back home by his side. He would take his small family to dine at the Royal Hotel, and they holidayed in Wiltshire, in Blackpool, and at Ballater near Balmoral where there was some sort of family connection. This wonderful existence was about to be shattered, however. William had been increasingly unwell – at one point, in an attempt to recuperate, he'd gone to stay with one of his brothers in Birmingham – and in April 1921 he died in the Derbyshire Royal Infirmary from a brain tumour; he was fifty-two.

Frank naturally saw a chance to bring better times to the rest of his family and set about taking over his brother's insurance business. My real grandfather lived until I was sixteen, and only a few streets away at that, but I probably never met him. My mother said that she refused to speak to her natural father ever again, never forgiving him for moving so swiftly to take over her adopted father's business before he was even in his grave.

She was only eight years old when Frank came to the tobacconist's shop to collect William's insurance books. She was hurt and angry and, to make her point, she jumped on Frank's bowler hat before running off down Abbey Street. It wasn't the last time she ran away from him. The following year Jane Rowley became ill and returned to her London roots to rest. My mother, meanwhile, was sent to stay with two of her sisters who were by now living with their Aunt Annie at 62 Friar Gate where Annie was housekeeper to a Miss Moseley, a lady of independent means. The idea was that my mother should eventually return to her natural father. Miss Moseley favoured young Phyllis above the others and allowed her to visit the large house's private quarters to handle fine china and jewellery, privileges denied her sisters. They retaliated by locking my mother, who was now nine years old, in a cellar, to be released only when Miss Moseley wondered where she was. Eventually, her father came to take her back to his new home. Once outside, however, she wrestled free and ran back to Abbey Street where a kindly neighbour took her in. There she remained until her adopted mother returned from London. To his credit, Frank Rowley, having seen the utter futility of it all, had allowed her to stay.

I say I probably never met my grandfather but one Saturday evening when I was about nine, my mother and I were waiting for my father at the corner of Friar Gate and Stafford Street – my father had a part-time job as a tote operator at the dog track in Vernon Street – when an elderly gentleman, a small figure wearing a bowler hat, three-piece suit and a gold watch chain, came up and spoke to her. The conversation lasted for only a few minutes. Then he patted me on the head, gave me a half-crown and walked off up Friar Gate. Years later, when I learned that my grandfather had lived in that area until he died, I couldn't help but wonder if some brief reconciliation had taken place that night. There was no reason for a complete stranger to give a small boy such a tidy sum of money, as a half-crown was in those days. Then again, my mother never gave the slightest hint that all had been forgiven. In fact, all things considered she could be a very unforgiving sort of person. She certainly remained effectively estranged from her three sisters and it was only in the mid-1990s that I met several cousins of whose existence I'd previously been unaware. Three sets of grandparents, me my own second cousin . . . no wonder I've always found life so bewildering.

So my mother returned to the tobacconist's shop in Abbey Street, to be brought up in 1920s Derby in a single-parent family, albeit one that enjoyed a fair amount of wealth compared with what she might have experienced had things turned out differently. The business continued to prosper and there were regular visits to the Grand Theatre in Babington Lane, and to the Royal Hotel for dinner, sometimes in the company of the man everyone called Cousin Fred. For years after the Second World War, Cousin Fred was an enigmatic figure in our family. There were photographs of him at his rubber planter's house in Malaya in the 1920s. We had the pictures that he'd painted behind the shop in Abbey Street just after the First World War, and rolls of beautiful silks that he'd sent from the Far East, still wrapped in brown paper on which exotic postage

Fred Densham relaxing at his rubber plantation in Johore in the 1930s. My mother turned down an invitation to join her cousin in Malaya. (Author's Collection)

stamps were affixed, the paper still bearing the traces of red sealing wax. In 1935, Fred had given my mother away at her wedding at St Chad's Church in New Normanton. Yet, as I grew up in Derby in the 1940s and 1950s, my mother would often say, to nobody in particular, 'I wonder whatever happened to Cousin Fred.'

Fred Densham was born in Wandsworth towards the end of 1890. In February 1908 he joined the Army. He was under age but added a few months and enlisted in the 5th Royal Irish Lancers at Fulford Barracks, York. The regiment moved to Ireland but, whenever he was on leave, Fred would always come to Derby to see his Aunt Jane. On the outbreak of war in August 1914, the Lancers were sent to France as part of the British Expeditionary Force. Corporal Densham was by now a signaller in 4th Troop. Alas, his war was short and not very sweet. Fred's first taste of action was in that hot August during the Battle of Mons, where he took part in rearguard actions in support of the retreating British forces. Two months later he was wounded and captured near the vital railway junction at Hazebrouck in northern France. Just over the Belgian frontier, Fred's unit had come into contact with German cavalry and, for Cousin Fred, the war was over – although at least he was still alive: two fellow lancers were killed and their heads and arms cut off. Fred spent the next four years as a POW at Doberitz, near Berlin. Released at the Armistice in

November 1918, he rejoined his regiment at the Curragh, from where he was demobbed. It was early 1919 and he made straight for Derby. Sitting in a shed at the top of the garden in Abbey Street, he began to paint. First a beautiful representation of the 5th Royal Irish Lancers crest, then a poignant picture of a First World War soldier with his horse. He called it 'Pals!' He was a versatile artist who could paint in both oils and watercolour, and in several different styles. Another of his works, a charming little cartoon, sits on my desk.

In September 1920, Fred sailed for Malaya. After the war, the rubber industry there was booming and hundreds of former British soldiers went out to seek a new life. Fred became an assistant planter on the island of Penang; by 1927 he was working in Kedah. He returned to England frequently, always to Derby to stay in Abbey Street. On each visit he took his Aunt Jane and cousin Phyllis to dinner at the Royal Hotel. On one occasion he went to America and came back on the *Queen Mary* in the company of the film star Boris Karloff. Apparently Fred knew how to enjoy himself. In 1932 he asked my mother to accompany him back to Malaya, to start a new life. She was not quite twenty, he was forty-two. Whether there was any romantic intention on Fred's part (they were cousins but not blood relatives), I have no idea. Nor do I know if she considered it for long, or rejected the idea out of hand. Somehow, I couldn't see her in the tropics, although the idea of servants must have appealed. Either way, it was a blessing that she didn't accept because ultimately she would have become swept up in one of the most horrific episodes of the twentieth century. In 1939 another world war came and with it the never-ending question, 'Whatever happened to Cousin Fred?' By 1941, Fred was managing a rubber plantation in Johore. When the Japanese invaded, he joined the Johore Volunteer Engineers as 51-year-old Sapper 1204 Densham. After fighting a rearguard action from Malaya across the causeway into Singapore, the JVE were captured in February 1942. Paraded on the Padang, a green open space in the centre of Singapore city, they were then force-marched to the internment camp at Changi. That was the last my mother heard of him

Obviously, if she had taken Fred up on his offer to begin a new life on the other side of the world, my mother wouldn't have met my father. And I wouldn't be writing this book. Alec Rippon came from the Lincolnshire fens. He'd worked on the *Lincolnshire Free Press*, the *Leicester Mail* and the *Hertfordshire Advertiser* before, in August 1929, obtaining a position at the paper's new offices in the former corn exchange and music hall in Albert Street, on the weekly wage of £4 3s 6d. He found lodgings with a man called Mycroft who lived at the bottom end of Gerard Street, where it joined Macklin Street. His fellow lodgers were a peculiar bunch; one of them liked a drink or several, and in the small hours of the morning he would awaken the whole household to warn them that 'blue demons' were afoot. My father soon settled in Derby, however. For one thing they had a decent football team and at every opportunity he was off to the Baseball Ground to watch Sammy Crooks, Jack Bowers, Dally Duncan and the rest of those pre-war Derby County heroes. For another, the town boasted a racecourse on Nottingham Road, and was soon to open a greyhound stadium at the old county gaol, site of all those public hangings. If there was one thing my father liked it was a gamble, and to live in a town that had its own horse and greyhound racing facilities must have seemed like heaven to him. Cricket, too, offered him plenty of recreation. Besides keeping wicket for the *Evening Telegraph* team, he could also watch Derbyshire who were then one of the best teams in the County Championship. Residing in Derby in the 1930s was a paradise for anyone interested in sport.

According to my mother, she met my father outside Woolworths in Victoria Street after he rescued her from the attentions of a man who was bothering her. Life is full of remarkable twists of fate; if Alec Rippon had walked past two minutes earlier, then he almost certainly wouldn't have met Phyllis Rowley and, from that seemingly insignificant fact, so many lives would ultimately have been completely different. Even so, quite how Alec and Phyllis got together is a marvel all on its own. They never appeared to have anything in common except to irritate each other; yet they were married in 1935, renting a flat in Gower Street. Two years later, they were on their way to Hull.

CHAPTER THREE

Dodgy Coalmen, Mad Butchers

I wasn't old enough to realise it at the time but the winter of 1946/7 was one of the worst in living memory: three months of thick snow and sub-zero temperatures followed by floods and gale-force winds. There was also a severe shortage of fuel with daily power cuts affecting homes and businesses alike. Unsurprisingly, it was also a winter that entered local folklore, in our neighbourhood at least, to be fondly recalled along with tales of the Blitz. I heard the stories hundreds of times and when it came to accounts of people struggling through 6ft of snow to the gas works in Ford Street, then pushing home a pramful of coke, I became as word perfect as those who'd actually done it. The winter apparently began with the sort of December fog that was to become a feature of growing up in industrial Britain after the Second World War. Every winter, fog, or rather smog, polluted everything it enveloped, a thick yellow cloud clinging to your clothes, searching your lungs. When the wind dropped and the air grew damper, it created fog; the smog element was added by the smoke from thousands of coal fires burning in domestic grates all over Derby, adding to the filth already rising from the town's factory chimneys. For housewives, it became pointless to put washing out to dry because it came in dirtier than when it went into the dolly tub. One of my earliest childhood memories is of having a bad cold and coughing up black-flecked phlegm. Every time you blew your nose you finished up with a handkerchief full of soot. There was an advertisement in Violet Craven's shop on the opposite corner of Webster Street to our house. It hung there for years after the war: 'Give Your Cold a Cephos Reception For Quick Relief.' Cephos was sold in tablet or powder form and cost 'twopence a dose including purchase tax'. The advertisement added, reassuringly, 'Cephos Does Not Affect The Heart'. It didn't mention whether it had any effect on sooty tonsils.

In the mid-1950s, smokeless zones were introduced and it became illegal to burn coal to heat homes; once that happened, then everyone's lung capacity began to improve. In the meantime, postwar British school-children grew up inhaling this noxious substance that must have been at least as bad as passive smoking, something to which I was exposed daily. About 75 per cent of adults regularly smoked. People smoked at work, at home, in the cinema, down the pub, on public transport. One of my earliest memories of floodlit football at the Baseball Ground is of thousands of cigarettes glowing in the darkened stands. Abstainers just had to lump it. I grew up in a house full of tobacco fumes. My father smoked cigarettes and a pipe – St Bruno tobacco for his briar and either John Player's Navy Cut or Gold Flake cigarettes. He was never without one or the other and could smoke a cigarette down to the tiniest nub. Still alight, it stuck to his bottom lip and wobbled up and down when he spoke.

My mother smoked cigarettes, originally Senior Service before moving on to something called Consulate; as she pointed out, they had a mentholated tip so, far from being harmful, they must actually be doing her good. Phil Vidofsky lit one cigarette from another as he cut hair at his barber's shop, first in Abbey Street, then later on the corner of Gerard Street and Wilson Street. Ted Barker, a butcher whose shop was at the top of Gerard Street, smoked as he prepared Sunday joints, his fingers stained brown by nicotine, ash falling on the meat. Nobody seemed to mind. Teachers smoked. A pupil entering the staff room at Bemrose School may as well have been standing in a back-street bookmakers on Grand National Day. Even doctors smoked. Dr Milburn, a GP at the surgery that used to stand in Leopold Street, conducted an examination of my throat while drawing on a small cigar and then blowing the smoke over me. 'If I give him something for this, it'll get better in two weeks; if you let nature take its course, it'll be gone in a fortnight', he told my mother between drags on a Will's Whiff. She inhaled some of her mentholated cigarette and nodded wisely while, outside, all the sick people waiting their turn coughed and hacked away in a fug of tobacco smoke. It's a wonder that anyone survived the postwar years.

Phil Vidofsky's barber's shop on the near corner of Wilson Street and Gerard Street with Brewin's paper shop on the other side of the street. (Author's Collection)

The view down Gerard Street from our front step. The pig bin was sited against the lamp-post on the right-hand side. This picture was taken in 1979, just before much of the area was demolished. (Author's Collection)

Smokers or non-smokers, our neighbourhood was a friendly place. Gerard Street ran from Macklin Street, at the town centre end, up to Burton Road which was then exactly what its name implied: the main road to Burton upon Trent. Gerard Street had been on the map of Derby since the 1840s, named, along with some of the streets off it – Macklin, Wilson and Rosengrave – after members of the family of an Irish-born vicar who apparently owned most of the land in what was the Newlands. The area was gradually developed, the terrace row that included our house being built in the 1880s. It had remained the same for well over half a century. Even in the 1940s and '50s there were still hardly any cars parked in Gerard Street, the only real hazard to a game of football or cricket being the pig bin by the lamp-post six doors from our house, outside what was still referred to as 'the Ship', even though the pub of that name had been converted to a private dwelling during the First World War. People talk about recycling as though it's a new idea but during the war, and in the days of severe rationing that followed it, households were encouraged to put their waste food into the public bins that were dotted around every street. The food went for animal feed, hence the name 'pig bin'. The bin nearest to our house served as a useful wicket for a game of street cricket, until one of us knocked it over that is: then everyone scattered rather than have the responsibility of collecting up the cabbage stalks, potato peelings and other rotting food rubbish that was strewn across the pavement. Arthur Smith, who lived at the Ship house, must have dreaded the light nights.

Arthur was just one of our neighbours. In the twenty-first century, it's not uncommon to live in a house for years and still know very little about your neighbours, sometimes not even the names of people who live only a few doors away. I knew practically everyone in Gerard Street, from top to bottom. Next door to us lived a widow, Mrs Orme, and her daughter and son-in-law, Nancy and Peter Warner. Nancy was a popular face on the cosmetics counter at Boot's the Chemist's main branch on the corner of East Street and St Peter's Street. Peter, a shy, gentle man, worked as a garage mechanic in Becket Street, a few minutes' walk from their house. He'd served in the RAF during the war and sported a handlebar moustache to prove it, although I think he was more ground crew than fighter pilot. On summer evenings he and Nancy would climb into their open-top sports car, Peter wearing a cravat, Nancy dolled up to the nines, and off they'd roar. Pubs in Derby closed at 10 p.m., but those in Derbyshire enjoyed an extra half-hour's drinking time; and as the town boundary then ended at the ring road, our neighbours didn't have to drive far in order to pull in an extra thirty minutes' pub time in those pre-Breathalyzer days.

In contrast to Peter and Nancy, who went out most evenings, across the road Mrs Brough seemed to spend her entire life standing on the front step of her house at number 92, bidding a cheery good morning or good afternoon to every passer-by. I don't ever remember walking up Gerard Street without receiving a beaming smile and a 'Hello my duck; how are you?' from Mrs Brough. My mother liked Mrs Brough and spent a fair amount of time gossiping with her. She was also good friends with one of her daughters, Gladys, who worked on the sweet counter at Woolworths in Victoria Street. One day we were walking through Woolies and stopped to speak to Gladys. Only after we'd left the store did my mother realise, to her horror, that her friend had slipped me a bag of sweets. Her first instinct was to go back and pay for them, but that might have landed Gladys in trouble. She took so long wrestling with the dilemma that, before she could reach a conclusion, I'd solved her problem by eating the evidence.

My two best friends were John Burns and Colin Shaw. They were both older than me: John was born in September 1940 during the Battle of Britain (which explains why his second name is Winston, after the prime minister of the day); Colin in March 1942. John lived at 16 Webster Street, the little dead-end road on whose corner our house sat. His father Tom was employed at the railway works; again, my mother was friendly with John's mother, Miriam. My mother suffered from periodic bouts of agoraphobia and I've known times when she would hardly leave the house for a year or more. Then it would suddenly disappear – there must have been an explanation but I never found out what it was – and there were times when she and Mim, as she called John's mum, would go out for a drink together. I spent a lot of time at number 16, although I was terrified of the Burnses' dog, a little terrier called Bobby, who was always growling, snapping and circling you while he weighed up your ankles. They had a wind-up gramophone and on wet afternoons John and I would crank it up and put on a 78rpm record. Oddly, the only one I can ever remember playing is the overture to *The Pirates of Penzance*.

My two best pals, John Burns (left) and Colin Shaw, both seated on a Derby Carnival float advertising CWS football boots sponsored by Stanley Matthews. It was the nearest they ever got to the maestro. (Colin Shaw)

I regarded John as an older brother as he was four years my senior. He was old enough to own an air-rifle and some afternoons in the school holidays we'd take potshots at the roofs of houses in Rosengrave Street (their gardens backed on to those of the houses in Webster Street). The pellets made a sort of pinging scream as they ricocheted off the roof slates, rather like those you heard in a western film. Amazingly, hardly anyone complained. Imagine trying that today. There'd be a police helicopter clattering overhead and Mr and Mrs Burnses' garden would be surrounded by armed officers while a voice on a loudhailer would be ordering you to come out with your hands in the air. Back in the early 1950s, the most that I can ever remember happening was a chap sticking his head over a garden wall, shaking a fist and yelling, 'Oi, clear off with your bloody air rifle or you'll get a clip round the ear!' He obviously didn't feel threatened. The same could be said of a game we played called wall-hopping. The idea was to go down someone's entry on a winter's evening (for obvious reasons it had to be dark) and into their garden, then to see how far we could get by climbing over garden walls before we emerged up an entry further down the street. The challenge was the thing. We were always very careful not to cause any damage (although one night someone jumped over a wall into Sam Bonnington's garden and put their foot through a cold frame that hadn't been there earlier in the week). Again, though, imagine finding strange figures in your garden these days; you'd fear for your life.

Near Christmas, John decided that we could liberate some holly from a large tree in the garden of Christ Church vicarage in Swinburne Street. It seemed fair enough: the tree was loaded with berries and the vicar was hardly going to miss a few sprigs. John's scheme involved sending someone over the fence and into the vicar's garden. They would then cut the holly and pass it over the fence to the waiting gang. All this seemed a good idea. The only part I didn't like was the bit where it was me who climbed over the fence. 'It's the most sensible thing to do', explained John, 'because if you get caught, as you're the youngest, he'll almost certainly let you go.' Almost certainly . . . I wasn't convinced but, desperately wanting to be a team player, I allowed myself to be lifted up and pushed over the vicar's fence. I'd been at work for about five minutes, snipping away with a pair of Mrs Burns's kitchen scissors, when a light came on in the vicar's kitchen and then the back door opened and a small

Atten . . . shun! Boyhood pals Colin Shaw (saluting), John Burns (right) and Keith Wilkinson in John's backyard at the top of Webster Street. (Colin Shaw)

dog appeared. I'd never got on with dogs – Bobby had seen to that – and now I feared the worst. Thankfully, this particular canine was no tracker dog. It seemed to resent being pushed out on a cold winter night and, after a cursory sniff around the nearest tree, it shot back into the house. The door closed, the light went out and I breathed again. I was, though, in no mood to continue stealing holly. But I had a problem: the garden was lower than the pavement and I couldn't climb back. Eventually I found a large plant pot which I rolled to the fence. I managed to heave myself back into the street which, of course, was now deserted, everyone else having fled at the first sign of trouble. I caught up with them under a street lamp in Gerard Street. John was sympathetic but a little disappointed. 'I thought you might have brought the holly you'd already got', he said. I was far too young to say the rude word that was forming in my brain.

Colin Shaw lived at 142 Gerard Street with his parents, Arthur and Dolly. The Shaws also had an older son, John, who was serving in the Korean War and who later suffered a terrible motor-cycle accident when called back for reservist training; happily, he survived, although badly injured. Arthur worked at Rolls-Royce, Dolly as a cleaner at the City Hospital. Again, their door was always open so far as I was concerned. Colin had a Subbuteo table football pitch on which we played for hours in his front room. In those days front rooms were hardly ever used; they were usually unheated, smelled of over-ripe fruit and, for some reason, always contained a china cabinet. But Dolly always lit the gas fire for us and it provided a cosy haven on dark winter's nights. We became quite inventive with the Subbuteo pitch, building stands and terraces out of old shoe boxes and even staging 'floodlit' matches by switching off the main light and tying bicycle lamps to empty pop bottles. The most wonderful part of the Shaws' house, though, was Arthur's garden shed, which had started off as an Anderson air-raid shelter. These were made from six curved corrugated iron sheets, bolted together at the top, with steel plates at either end, and measuring 6ft 6in by 4ft 6in. The shelters, which could accommodate six people, were originally half buried in the ground with earth heaped on top. Their entrances were protected by a steel shield and an earthen blast wall. When the war ended, Arthur, like tens of thousands of others, turned his air-raid shelter into a shed. For two young lads with a vivid imagination this became the cockpit of a Lancaster bomber on a dangerous mission over Berlin, the hull of a submarine searching for German shipping in the North Atlantic, a machine-gun emplacement in the Western Desert. We must have spent hundreds of hours in that shed, happily fighting the Second World War all over again.

As we all grew older, sex and the production of babies inevitably became a major topic of conversation. There wasn't the remotest chance that anyone's parents were going to give their offspring a lecture on the birds and the bees – this was the early 1950s, remember – and so ignorance on our part led to a number of wild rumours circulating. One that I recall thinking must be unlikely was that if the baby didn't receive enough seed, then it would grow up to be a cripple. Another, which sounded more promising, was that once a woman became pregnant, every few days her husband had to 'top up' the baby growing inside her. By this time, we had at least grasped the rudiments of sex, thanks to John Burns. One day he announced that on the coming Friday, his class at Rykneld School was to be given a sex education lesson. Colin and I were waiting outside his house when John pulled up on his bike after school. He related what he'd been told and then we departed because Colin had to run an errand for his mother. I went with him and we walked up Harcourt Street to the Co-op on Burton Road. Eventually, it was me who broke the silence.

'What do you think? You know, about what John just said?'

Colin, who attended Green Hill Methodist Chapel in St Peter's Churchyard, furrowed his brow. 'Personally, I don't believe it. I've been thinking about it, and I just can't see our minister doing anything like that.' That was good enough for me.

I was in my first year at grammar school before anyone attempted to give me an official sex education lesson. It was promised by a science teacher called Bill Spencer who'd served as a lieutenant in the Notts and Derby Regiment during the First World War. The day came and we filed expectantly into the Pasteur laboratory. Bill hurried in behind us, flustered and obviously embarrassed by the whole thing. 'I am instructed by the education authority to tell you about sex and reproduction,' he announced apologetically. We sat with bated breath while he told us about frog spawn. After touching briefly on the reproductive organs of rabbits (with the aid of a diagram that may as well have been a plan of a household boiler), he obviously felt he'd gone as far as public decency would allow. He snapped shut the book he'd been clutching and told us that we could begin that evening's homework. Thank goodness for the enlightened Rykneld School, and for John Burns for sharing the information.

Next door but one to John lived a family called the Wilkinsons. There were three brothers and the middle one, Keith, was nearest in age to John, Colin and me. Keith hung around with us occasionally but, more often than not, seemed to plough his own furrow. Our happy gang was complemented by several girls who were an integral part of the games we played – the obvious hide and seek (Colin and I insisted on blackening our faces with soot and turning it into a commando raid), and something called 'squashed tomato' about which I can remember absolutely nothing except that it involved the most complicated set of rules imaginable. Kathleen Radford, whose father, Cyril, was one of two local window cleaners (George Manning was the other), was a regular as were Janet Foster, who lived in Webster Street, Eileen Pople, who also lived in Webster Street and was to marry John Burns, and Margaret Helliwell, who lived opposite us. Margaret's father, Fred, was a bit of a card. Every evening at 7.30 p.m. prompt Fred would emerge from his house, glance at his watch, and, looking most reluctant, stroll off to the Durham Ox, a large white-tiled nineteenth-century pub that stood on the corner of Gerard Street and Burton Road. Fred always had this 'oh well, I suppose I must' manner when he set off to the pub. As he crossed the road by our house, he'd wink and ask, 'Are you coming for one, then?' The funny thing was, he never asked me once I'd turned eighteen, a fact I often put to him in the ensuing years. Susan and Pat Mellor, who lived just up the road, also joined in our games, although Pat, the older sister, eventually found more sophisticated companions. Doris Wass, who lived with her parents at the first house in Webster Street, also went her own way for much of the time. Doris and I were the only kids in the neighbourhood to pass our eleven-plus exam – Doris went to Homelands, one of two girls' grammar schools in Derby – and eventually she developed an interest in Derby County so we went to a few reserve-team matches together before she found other pursuits.

None of the girls, though, were involved in an incident that one afternoon left John gasping for breath, and Colin and me crying with laughter. The three of us were hoofing a tennis ball to one another across Gerard Street when a hearse, empty except for the driver, came around the corner. John decided that he could probably kick the ball under the vehicle as it passed us, but unfortunately he was no Stanley Matthews (none of us were) and instead he hammered it against the driver's door. The hearse pulled up sharply and out sprang the driver. The three of us scattered in different directions and the irate driver elected to chase John. For some reason he collected his top hat as he leapt from the hearse. It was the most comical sight imaginable, our pal fleeing down Colin's entry with a top-hat-carrying funeral director close behind. Now assured that we were safe, Colin and I stopped running and began to laugh; we laughed until we cried, chests heaving, hands on our knees, tears streaming down our faces. Twenty minutes later, peeking through the

Shaws' front-room curtains, we saw the red-faced hearse driver return, still clutching his topper. He fell back into his vehicle and sat there for a full five minutes, regaining his composure before driving off. Another half-hour elapsed and then John also reappeared, furtively making his way back down the street in case funeral man was lying in wait. Apparently he'd pursued John over two garden walls, across Abbey Street and right up Stockbrook Street before finally giving up the chase.

Tangling with motor traffic was unusual. Few neighbours owned a car and even some tradesmen relied on a more sedate mode of transport. Bailey's greengrocer's, whose shop was on the corner of Macklin Street and Becket Street, used a horse and cart to make deliveries. Old man Bailey sat atop the cart, the reins casually draped over one finger as the horse trotted purposefully up the street; the animal obviously knew its way. Occasionally it would decide to take a toilet break in the road outside our house, which would be the signal for a frantic scramble between two neighbours, George Green and Walter Boaler, each of whom would appear carrying a bucket and shovel: horse manure was a vital ingredient for the rivals' prize roses, or was it rhubarb?

Abbey Street coalman Bill Boden also used genuine horsepower and taking delivery of the household coal was a vital job, not least because my mother suspected that our particular coalman was something of a cheat. As soon as I'd learned to count, I was posted at the front door to supervise the coal going into our cellar, with strict instructions to count every bag. And even when the correct number of bags had been confirmed, there were still arguments over the quality of the coal itself, with allegations that much of it was 'slack' – loose chippings mixed with coal dust rather than good-sized lumps. Like food and clothing, coal was rationed and each family had to be registered with a particular coalman. After my mother fell out with our coal merchant, she worked her way through several others. Every one of them was suspected of short measure, dropping a bag short, or making up the load with inferior stuff. Eventually, she accepted that they were all much of a muchness, some worse than others but none scrupulously honest, so she gave up changing coalman – actually, I think she would have been round to the first one again – although the ritual of counting the bags continued.

It wasn't just coalmen who upset my mother. We were registered with a butcher called Donald Sims whose shop was in Abbey Street. He was an odd sort of cove who would suddenly start shouting and banging things about in the middle of serving his customers. I rather liked him because he didn't really seem like a normal adult. One day we were queuing up for some sausages when he suddenly flung a meat cleaver over the queue and into the wall. 'That'll wake you up', he roared. My mother immediately declared him insane and stalked out. A few days later we were registered with Wilf Sharman who had premises further down Abbey Street. Wilf was a nice enough chap, but far too normal for my liking. In the ten years we patronised his shop I never once saw him threaten to decapitate a customer.

Corner shops, though, were the life-blood of the community. Apart from Violet Craven's little operation, which I think was more of a hobby than an income (her husband, Ernie, worked at Rolls-Royce), we mostly

Violet Craven's shop on the corner of Webster Street and Gerard Street just before it was pulled down. It was a great place for a chat. (Author's Collection)

used a general grocer's which stood on the corner of Gerard Street and Grey Street. Over the years it had a number of owners after Sylvia, my godmother, left. Eric Addelsee and his wife ran it for a while in the mid-1950s. They had a daughter called Marie, who was five years older than me and became lumbered with taking me to the Saturday children's picture show at the Alexandra cinema on Normanton Road. The Alex was unusual in that its kids' shows were screened in the afternoons rather than in the mornings, as happened at the Black Prince, in Colyear Street, and at other cinemas in the town. The Addelsees left to run a shop at Sunnyhill (the Alex closed down soon afterwards, to become the Trocadero dance hall which, in turn, burned down) and their place was taken by a Mrs Harrison and her daughter and son-in-law. Mrs Harrison was an attractive woman who soon gained an admirer, a former Italian prisoner-of-war called Alberto who lived in Harcourt Street. Alberto, who sported a thin moustache which he kept jet black with some kind of dye, and who absolutely reeked of garlic, wooed Mrs Harrison, unsuccessfully alas, from the day she arrived in Gerard Street until the day she left. He could never quite get my name right and would scurry past me, booming out "'Ello, Tony!' as he went. Mrs Harrison was followed by Ken Tipping and his wife, and then Owen Hobday and his wife. They were all good people, always ready to give someone a helping hand in an emergency, or offer the use of their telephone, for few households boasted one. I was rather more wary of Harry Wallis, who ran an off-licence on the opposite corner of Grey Street. Harry, a large, ruddy-faced man who always wore a brown smock, was not into small talk with children. On Monday evenings he took a night off and could be seen striding up Harcourt Street, trilby hat set at a jaunty angle, on his way to the second house at the

The off-licence at the bottom of Forester Street with its politically incorrect advertisement for Kimberley ale. It showed a stereotyped figure of a little black boy in a turban. (Author's Collection)

Hippodrome Theatre. I expect he was a nice chap really but he always struck me as being a bit sharp, certainly compared to the succession of shopkeepers on the other side of the street.

Harry Wallis's was one of three off-licences in Gerard Street which also boasted two pubs. While the Durham Ox, run by Joe Kent, stood at the Burton Road end, the Marquis of Granby was next to Becket School. Occasionally my father would run out of cigarettes and I'd be sent to the little 'snug' at the Marquis, a tiny room not much bigger than a telephone box, to fetch emergency supplies. The snug opened directly on to the street and there was a bench seat upon which there always seemed to be the same three old ladies with their bottles of milk stout. They summoned fresh drinks by tapping on an opaque glass window, the point being that they liked a drink but didn't want to be seen actually sitting in a pub. On summer evenings Ernie Craven would stroll down to the Marquis, fill up a big white enamel jug with draught bitter, then return up the street, being careful not to spill a drop, for a night by the wireless with Violet.

In the mid-1950s our first black neighbours arrived. Previously, the only non-white people I'd seen had been a couple of black GIs from the American army camp at Marchington, a West Indian bus conductor in Nottingham when we went to a Test match, and a door-to-door brush salesman who wore a turban and occasionally visited houses in our street. Now Steve Parboo, himself a West Indian, had taken over 137 Gerard Street, a large house which had previously been run by Mrs Watkins who took in lodgers. Steve also ran a guest house for his fellow countrymen who were arriving in Derby in increasing numbers. He always seemed to be wearing a smile and was a great cricket fan, so we always had a natter when we bumped into each other. Britain was still coming to terms with non-white immigration and there were some ridiculous stories doing the rounds, such as the new West Indian community were buying tinned cat food for themselves to eat. When people started arriving from the Indian

The Marquis of Granby pub in Gerard Street, another Derby hostelry that was demolished by the council. (Author's Collection)

sub-continent, a rumour quickly took hold that they would buy a house in a row of terraces, then knock through the wall into the next-door loft, and so on. Then the story was elaborated to have some white resident about ten houses away opening his loft to find a family of Indians or Pakistanis bedded down above his own bedroom. It was all pure nonsense, of course, but that didn't prevent some neighbours from repeating it as if it was a well-established fact.

Those first non-white immigrants (Derby already had plenty of Poles and Italians) came to work in heavy industrial factories like International Combustion, Leys and Qualcast, and they often clubbed together to buy the big houses in Rosehill Street and the surrounding area. The complexion of that neighbourhood began to alter quickly. Where doctors, dentists and the town's major business proprietors had once lived, now it was the home of families from the Caribbean (for some reason they were all known as 'Jamaicans' even though some must have come from other islands), India and Pakistan, whose menfolk mostly worked as labourers or in other menial jobs that white people didn't particularly want to do (that didn't prevent whites from occasionally going on strike when a non-white person was given a job in their factory). It was an area I already knew well as it lay directly on my route to the Baseball Ground. One Saturday afternoon I was astonished to see hundreds of Asian men sitting in little groups on Arboretum Field playing cards. It felt like an invasion and the initial resentment from many of the indigenous population was understandable enough. The smell of curry (ironically now practically Britain's national dish) could be quite nauseating to people brought up on a bland diet of meat and two veg, although exposure to Alberto's garlic had inured me to it. Unlike the West Indians, hardly any of the immigrants from the sub-continent could speak English and, in the end, it became more a matter of culture than of colour. Yet some people will always be prejudiced, no matter what, and there were many who never

Not the opening shot from Coronation Street *but a 1960s aerial view from the tower of St Luke's Church in Stockbrook Street, across the area in which I grew up. St Alkmund's Church and Derby Power Station can be seen in the distance. (Author's Collection)*

accepted non-white people. West Indians actually fitted in rather more easily than Indians or Pakistanis. For a start we could understand them. And a lot of them went to Christian churches (rather more often than most of the locals, it has to be said). In short, their behaviour was familiar and recognisable. Most prejudice is born of ignorance.

When a Chinese family moved into Gerard Street, a few doors down from us, we had a new problem. Until the 1960s, few private homes boasted a telephone; in an emergency we usually went to the corner shop and paid to use their phone. Eventually I had one installed at home so that my duties as a football club secretary could be carried out more easily. By now, many more people were buying telephones and there just weren't enough lines to go round so the GPO (yes, the British telephone system was once run by the General Post Office) invented something called 'party lines' where two houses shared the same line. The chances were that if you lifted the receiver to make a call, you'd find the other people gabbling away. Then you'd have to wait until they had finished and the only way to tell was to keep lifting your own receiver to check. Unfortunately we shared our party line with the Chinese family, which wouldn't ordinarily have been a problem had their children not invented a game that involved yelling down their phone. Many times one of us had to knock on their door and try to make the parents understand (they spoke absolutely no English) that their kids were messing about again. Normally, they just smiled and nodded, and then shut the door. Happily, the GPO eventually installed more lines and we stopped bothering our Chinese neighbours with mystifying gestures.

CHAPTER FOUR

Becket School . . . and a Coronation

In January 1950, I started school. It wasn't hard to find; it was only 100yd from our house. Gerard Street School was one of Derby's earliest 'board schools', built in Victorian times when a law was passed making free education available to all children up to the age of twelve. My mother had attended Gerard Street School between 1917 and 1926. Since then it had been renamed Becket School, after the council ward in which it stood, but I doubt the building itself had changed since it was opened in 1879. Big draughty classrooms, perilously steep steps leading down to a concrete playground that looked like a barrack square, and outside toilets that froze in winter – they all added up to something out of a Dickens novel. My first day at this grim, forbidding building was something of a trial because almost everyone else had enjoyed three months' start on me. As my birthday didn't fall until just before Christmas, I wasn't allowed to start at the beginning of the school year in September 1949. It was a crazy rule and I'd have been much better off going in with everyone else. As it was, they all knew the ropes and I had to catch up. It wasn't a matter of the lessons so much – for my age I was a good reader – but the day-to-day business of operating among one's peers. These days children are put into nurseries and kindergartens even before they can walk, so they can hone social skills from a very early age. Sixty years ago, such things didn't exist.

On that first day, a boy called Terry Tattershaw was put in charge of me. He was actually a lot smaller than me, but a kindly lad who steered me through. We remained good pals until the eleven-plus examination sent us on our different ways. Terry was universally known as 'Rags', not because his parents couldn't afford decent clothes for him but simply as a play on his surname. Another boy who became a good pal was Neil Heath who lived in Talbot Street. Richard Hawkridge was another. He lived at the bottom of Stockbrook Street and his mother and mine seemed to get on well. Like Rags, Neil and Richard went to a different school after the eleven-plus exam – still referred to in those days as 'the scholarship' – that was supposed to separate the bright kids from the rest. Of course, I was pleased enough eventually to be regarded as one of the brighter ones, but the exam was severely flawed, providing as it did a crossroads at such an early time in a child's development. There were plenty of kids who wasted their chance of a grammar school education, while many of those who

Most Derby children had their photographs taken at Jerome's in Victoria Street. Here I am with my mother in 1950, just after I started school. Note the Eagle *comic lapel badge. (Author's Collection)*

went to secondary modern school eventually did rather better. One such boy was Stanley Guy, a fair-haired lad who failed his eleven-plus; Stanley worked for the Foreign Office, then became an international banker, and later enjoyed a career as an author of thrillers set in Japan. Julian Grant, who lived in Macklin Street, was another who failed the exam but who went on to greater things. He joined the Merchant Navy as a radio officer and later became chairman of the Hydrographic Society. I haven't a clue what that is, but it sounds very impressive.

Miss Aiken, the headmistress of the infants' school in Gerard Street, was a tiny woman with a penchant for large hats bearing fruits and flowers. She was a relic of the days when female schoolmistresses had to remain spinsters or give up their jobs if they wed. Eventually, Miss Aiken did get married. In the meantime, she ran a tight ship at Becket School where, believe it or believe it not, we still used slates and chalk in the infants' class. The school was part of a bigger complex, backing on to what had been, until 1930, the Derby Municipal Secondary School for Boys. In that year, the Municipal School moved to new premises on Uttoxeter New Road, to become Bemrose Grammar School, which eventually allowed Abbey Street Girls' Secondary School to move into their part of the old building. The big girls' playground was where the infants from Gerard Street were shunted at playtime. At the age of eight, however, we graduated to the junior school which was part of the same building, and so we now had to take our chance in the juniors' playground. Lesson were basic but solid: arithmetic, including learning by rote the times tables until we possessed what amounted to a mental pocket calculator; reading and writing; history and geography. What more did we need? PT lessons were usually conducted outside, no matter what the weather, and the poorer kids had to make use of the plimsolls provided by the education authority; these were kept in the 'pump cage' and there were stories of all manner of diseases and terrible foot conditions caused by wearing communal footwear.

When we moved into the juniors, boys and girls were segregated, only to come together again in our last year at Becket Juniors. The education remained good and basic – the Three Rs taught in an old-fashioned way – but discipline could be harsh. The junior school headmaster, Bob Stanley, was one of the old brigade. He wasn't too bad – although he could still dish out the cane – but some of his teachers were to be feared. The worst of all was a chap called Widdowsen who, unfortunately, was my class teacher for two years. Widdowsen was bald and his whole head reminded me of a grinning skull. Only he didn't do all that much grinning. He had several party pieces, including strolling up to a desk and then bringing down a ruler on the knuckles of an unsuspecting child whose only offence might have been to let his gaze wander when he should have been trying to absorb the joys of long division. Worst of all, before our classes were streamed according to ability, I saw many instances where pupils who really should have been in a remedial group beaten for just not grasping what they were being told.

Becket School awaits demolition, not long after celebrating its centenary. It didn't look much more cheerful when I attended it. (Author's Collection)

Widdowsen's eyes really lit up when he could administer properly considered corporal punishment. Unlike his peremptory strikes with the ruler, canings gave him a moment to relish. There were two sorts of cane at Becket School, a whippy effort made of thin bamboo, and a thick stick. Both hurt like hell but the thicker version, which Widdowsen favoured, left the longer-lasting pain, like trapping your hand in a door. You could get yanked out for anything – talking, day-dreaming, even scratching your nose. Widdowsen's face would twist until it looked as though he was wearing some sort of maniacal mask, and then he would bring the cane down from a great height and with a follow-through that would have done justice to Len Hutton smiting Ray Lindwall through the covers. It was always on the hands, sometimes two strokes on each, and the trick was to drop your palm ever so slightly a split second before impact. If Widdowsen spotted you doing this, then the punishment was doubled, but it was worth the risk because the manoeuvre could cushion some of the pain. It still hurt a lot, however, and anyone with any pride would fight back the tears and resume their seat while trying to look as if it hadn't really hurt at all. Otherwise, Widdowsen had won. On one occasion a particularly nervous pupil removed his hand altogether which resulted in Widdowsen cracking the cane against his own knee. You can imagine what happened next.

There were some kind teachers, of course. Two of the younger ones – Mr Gathercole and Mr Warren – were my favourites. Both reasonable men who knew how to stimulate their pupils' interest, they made learning a delight. Mrs Townsend, who lived in Chatsworth Street by Normanton Park, was also an excellent teacher, even if her football coaching skills left something to be desired. In my first year at junior school, Mrs Townsend drew the short straw for taking us for games. Becket School had absolutely no sporting facilities and so we were marched to the nearest piece of grass which happened to be on Mill Hill Lane, in the grounds of Temple House, a Georgian building which, by the early 1950s, was being used as a remedial school. The set-up was strange, to say the least: what passed for a football pitch was actually L-shaped, so that one set of goalposts was at right-angles to the other. A buccaneering forward, who had broken away from the opposing defence, had to suddenly stop his run, put his foot on the ball and then turn a sharp right (or left, of course, depending on which end he was attacking) to continue towards goal. None of this bothered Mrs Townsend, who simply split us up into two teams – sometimes as many as twenty-a-side so it was quite possible to go through the entire afternoon without actually touching the ball – blew a whistle and then retired to the touchline to read a magazine. Eventually we were able to use the facilities at Rykneld Recreation Ground, although this meant wasting half the afternoon walking there and back, and we were also bussed to the old Derby racecourse where there were dozens of proper football pitches.

I enjoyed playing football, wherever we had to go to find a suitable pitch, but one activity with which I was less than enamoured was the Friday morning hymn practice which took up about two hours. A good solid Christian education was the basis for any British school in the 1940s

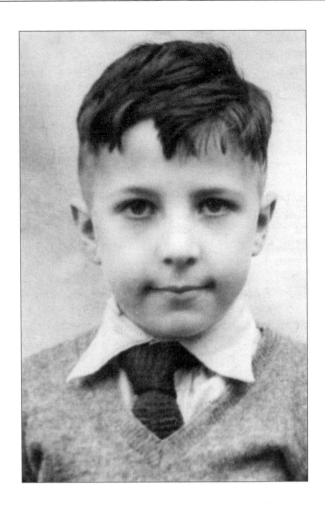

The school photographer arrived at Becket School in 1952. I wasn't fashion-conscious enough to tuck in my shirt collar. (Author's Collection)

and '50s, and I have always been grateful for the fact that, at grammar school, we had a proper religious service each morning. But two hours of hymn practice? Eventually I worked my ticket on that one. The whole of Thursday afternoons was given over to painting, and two volunteers were needed to clean up the following morning. Up shot a forest of hands and a boy called Roy Reed and I were selected, perhaps on the premise that neither of us could actually sing. Thereafter, Roy and I spent Friday mornings happily washing brushes and palettes to the muffled accompaniment of 'Onward Christian Soldiers'.

Roy and I were paint monitors, and we were also milk monitors, a post that, in October 1954, led to me being taken by ambulance to Derby Children's Hospital in North Street, after a large pane of glass fell out of a classroom door on to my head as we were delivering a crate of milk. It was one of those slow-motion moments; I watched in some fascination as the pane detached itself from the just-slammed door and fell towards me. I couldn't get out of the way, so I just waited for the impact, fortunately remembering to close my eyes at the very last second. Taken downstairs to the washrooms, I looked in a mirror to see that my face was covered in blood. At the Children's Hospital one of our kindly Leopold Street surgery GPs, Dr Eisenberg was on duty. First, slivers of glass were removed from my face and eyelids, then the crown of my head was stitched without the use of anaesthetic.

'I'm sorry but I can't give you an injection there', said Dr Eisenberg, 'so this might hurt a bit.' He was right and, to add insult to injury, the teacher who'd been deputed to accompany me was the dreaded Mr Widdowsen. With no transport available to take me home – the emergency was over, of course – we walked in total silence back to Gerard Street where my mother had just about recovered from being told by Roy Reed that 'there's been a terrible accident; Anton's head is hanging off'. Roy always seemed to be around when there were medical dramas. Once, he and I had to visit the school dentist together off Mill Hill Lane. We both had to have teeth extracted and sat there miserably looking at each other without saying a word as we waited, thick rubber aprons around our necks, for the dreaded gas mask to be applied. For some reason, the nasty little Scottish dentist couldn't get me to sleep. Or rather he couldn't keep me asleep because I woke up to find him wrestling with a stubborn molar. I panicked and tried to leave, which caused all kinds of problems. Eventually he managed to knock me out again and soon Roy and I were trudging back to school together, mouthfuls of cotton wool adding to two already mournful expressions.

So, there are more bad memories than good ones from my days at Becket School, but there was one real highlight: the Coronation of Queen Elizabeth II in June 1953. In February 1952, King George VI died. Along with other seven- and eight-year-olds I was sitting cross-legged on a canteen floor in Gerard Street when the BBC interrupted a schools wireless broadcast. John Snagge, more at home commentating on the Boat Race, began gravely, 'This is London. It is with the greatest sorrow that we make the following announcement . . .' When he'd finished, our teacher, Mrs Alright, said, also in a grave voice, 'Wait here. I must inform the headmaster.' It seemed important, so when I got home, I informed my mother, who didn't seem especially interested. She was one of the few people I knew who actively disliked the Queen Mother. The king's wife had told some of my mother's bombed-out Hull neighbours, 'My house has been bombed too, you know.' Buckingham Palace had just caught a stray German bomb, but my mother thought she was being patronising to people who'd lost everything. 'She had a choice of another six castles', she muttered every time she retold the story, which was often.

Indeed, the death of George VI, while greeted with general sadness, didn't impact directly on most people's lives. This was half a century before Elton John lamented Diana, Princess of Wales, and the perfume from the wall of flowers left at the gates of Kensington Palace could be smelt from a mile away; fifty years before every perceived indiscretion of a royal was splashed over the tabloid press. George VI had a special place in the hearts of the British people because of his role during the war, but royalty were still regarded as demi-gods who occasionally appeared on balconies to wave to the hoi polloi below. Deference was the general attitude. So when the king died, everyone felt it their duty to be sad, but without ever believing that it would make any difference to their own lives. It was, though, an excuse for pageantry. As the king lay in state in Westminster Hall, I leaned over our wireless set and listened to the voice of Richard Dimbleby: 'Never better, safer guarded, lay a sleeping king than this.' The day after the funeral, I pored over photographs published in the *Daily Mail*: the king's coffin draped in the Royal Standard, the Imperial State Crown, the Gold Orb, the Sceptre, the insignia of the Order of the Garter and a white wreath from the Queen Mother placed on top of the casket which was wheeled through London's streets on a gun carriage pulled by military personnel. At 2 p.m. on the day of the funeral, in Gerard Street the entire school had been assembled in the main hall to observe the two minutes' silence that had fallen over the United Kingdom and throughout the Commonwealth. I remember thinking that I was taking part in an historic occasion.

Coronation Day in Derby dawned wet and miserable. We went to school, each to receive our Coronation spoon, a gift from the Derby Borough Education Committee, and were then given the rest of the day off. Gerard Street didn't hold a party – although nearby Grey Street won a prize for the best-decorated street in the town – and instead we went to

On the day of George VI's funeral in 1952 we observed two minutes' silence at school. Here, Derby's civic leaders are pictured outside the Council House on their way to the cathedral for a service to mark the king's death. (Derby Evening Telegraph)

Bass's Rec to see the Coronation exhibition which included displays by the armed forces. My mother, who was by now displaying strong anti-royalist feelings – the Queen Mother really did have a lot to answer for – boycotted the festivities; she always seemed to want to swim against the tide. The exhibition included a large tent in which there were several television sets for us to watch the procession and ceremony in black and white; it would be a few weeks before I saw it in colour, with the rest of my classmates, at the Odeon in St Peter's Street, where the film *Elizabeth is Queen* was screened.

Black and white or colour, it made no difference to me because we didn't have a telly at home. Nor did many other people. Colin Shaw's parents owned a set, however, and a few weeks before the Coronation I'd joined other neighbours in the Shaws' crowded front room to watch the FA Cup Final, when Stanley Mortensen of Blackpool scored three goals but it became known as the Matthews Final. Most television sets had screens no more than 9in wide, set in a walnut cabinet so bulky that the screen looked even smaller; my pal John Cheadle's father used to watch the Cup Final on their television through a pair of binoculars. Eventually manufacturers began to sell magnifying screens which were supposed to make the picture larger but succeeded only in distorting it. Then came the first attempt at colouring television pictures. This, too, involved no great scientific breakthrough, just another screen to place in front of your set. This screen, though, had three coloured bands: blue at the top, brown in the middle, green at the bottom. It added a crude novelty value when film of the countryside was being shown; otherwise viewers had to get used to newsreaders and actors with blue hair, brown faces and green torsos.

Acting, with or without a brown face, has never interested me, but it was at Becket School that I made my one and only stage appearance, in a Christmas play written by one of the teachers who gave it the unlikely title of *Robin Hood Meets Father Christmas* (or it could have been the other way round; anyway, they met). I was given the part of Friar Tuck, which involved wearing a large dressing-gown stuffed with cushions and some pink headgear edged with brown paper to give the impression of a monk's haircut (twenty years later, I could have played the part without the disguise). I've no recollection of the plot, if indeed there was one. My only memories are of speaking the lines, 'There is the treasure', and then pointing dramatically to my left, only to discover that the boy deputed to bring a sack on stage had placed it to my right, contrary to everything that we had rehearsed; and of seeing the red, round and jolly face of Councillor Teddy Clay, father of my pal Stuart, roaring with laughter in the depths of the audience.

Finally, it was time to leave Becket Juniors. On a Thursday afternoon in March 1956, along with a dozen others, I was summoned to the headmaster's study. Normally, such an invitation would have evoked a sense of fear because it usually meant, at best, a telling-off and, at worst, a caning. But on this day I was unconcerned because most of my fellow pupils who accompanied me along the corridor towards Bob Stanley's office had never been in trouble in their lives. True, Stuart Clay, a fellow traveller when it came to sailing close to the wind, was in this little group.

But so, too, were Michael Wood and Anthony Trippett. If they were involved, then clearly we were going because it was good news. We entered individually, in alphabetical order, so I was some way down the list. Each boy and girl emerged clutching a brown envelope with strict instructions to deliver it to our parents unopened. I tore mine open the moment the bell went to end the day's lessons. Well before I'd completed the short journey home, I knew that I'd passed my eleven-plus and was going to grammar school. My father was still at work, but my mother was so pleased that she offered to pay for me and a friend to go to the pictures that evening – a hitherto unheard-of event in the middle of a school week – and I elected to take Colin Shaw, who was celebrating his fourteenth birthday, to the Black Prince in Colyear Street to see the wartime drama *The Man Who Never Was*.

There was a choice of boys' grammar schools: Derby School, founded in 1554 by Queen Mary as the Free Grammar School; and Bemrose, founded in 1930. My parents took advice from Alderman Alec Ling, a former mayor of Derby whose father, Oswald, had witnessed my mother's adoption papers forty-four years earlier. Alderman Ling recommended Bemrose. That suited me because the sports facilities there were much better than at Derby School, which was still housed in the eighteenth-century St Helen's House in the town centre. I've no recollection of the rest of my time at junior school. The summer term passed in a blur and in July my mother wheeled me off to John Manners in Green Lane to be kitted out in the maroon and white uniform of Bemrose School.

CHAPTER FIVE

Only Half a Mile Long

My mother often told me that Abbey Street was exactly a mile long. It was a claim made by neighbours, too, so I'd stand on Burton Road, look down to the far end of Abbey Street, and think, 'Well, that's what a mile looks like.' Small boys need to know these things. But small boys grow bigger and one day begin to question what adults have told them. So eventually I took a map and a ruler and discovered that, in fact, Abbey Street was nearer to half a mile long. I can still remember the dawning disappointment as I checked and rechecked my measurements. The distance that Roger Bannister had just covered in under four minutes suddenly took on a whole new picture in my mind. But a mile long, or only half a mile, Abbey Street was an important part of my life in Derby in the years after the war because it was a focal point of our daily existence, a street running like a main artery, coursing life into the veins of the smaller streets that ran off it, where housewives gossiped over the tight counters of corner shops.

It was those shops that gave Abbey Street its unique flavour. From Burton Road – where a peeling notice still advised horse drivers to slacken the reins when negotiating the hill – the street dropped sharply to where Boyer Street ran off to the left, leading away to Firs Estate. It was in Boyer Street that there was this wonderland of a shop. I was never quite sure what an emporium actually was, but I imagined that the establishment run by Tommy Harris, a well-known Derby magician, was as near to it as made no difference. For a start, Tommy's shop had a unique smell – soap, firewood, ironmongery and paraffin – and sold everything from dusters to dustbins, saucepans to steel wool. For another, Tommy would often buy a consignment of the most weird and wonderful things of no practical use to anyone save a child with a fevered imagination. I persuaded my mother to buy me a pith helmet from Tommy Harris's. Others followed suit and, that summer, a stranger might have wondered why all the small boys in that particular corner of Derby appeared to be on safari. On another occasion it was a job lot of naval hats; another time straight, high-sided fezzes that had been part of the parade uniform of the King's African Rifles. In fact, Tommy offered two sorts of fez because he also stocked a low version sported by the West African Frontier Force. Whatever had initially possessed him to buy up overstocks from Britain's fast-fading colonial armies I have no idea, but every time he quickly sold out.

Tommy Harris's shop in Boyer Street. He sold everything from paraffin to pith helmets. (Author's Collection)

Just to make a change from unusual hats, one day Tommy put in his window a display of thick bamboo poles. Again, they were of no real use but I invested sixpence in one which later served as a prop in more than a few battle re-enactments in Colin Shaw's backyard. Another boy from our neighbourhood, a cheerfully uncomplicated lad called Brian Price, also came into possession of one of these bamboo poles which were about 6ft long. One Saturday morning I was coming out through the revolving door of the Central Educational Company, which then traded at the bottom of St Peter's Street, when Brian came in the other way carrying his pole. He badly misjudged things and there was a horrendous splintering sound as the door swallowed up the bamboo. Of course, it didn't do the door much good either; in fact it jammed, trapping poor Brian inside. Fortunately, I'd managed to escape into the street a split second before the door ground to a halt, so I hung around for a while to watch him being rescued and then severely reprimanded. There he was, a crestfallen figure inspecting his chewed-up pole while the red-faced shop manager gave him a dressing-down and crowds of shoppers checked their stride to see what was going on. Brian, though, was a happy-go-lucky character and it wasn't long before he was off on some other daft adventure, his skirmish with the Central Ed's revolving door soon forgotten.

Brian lived somewhere near the Lord Belper beer house which stood on the corner of Spa Lane and Abbey Street. It was a pub that I never actually entered because it was demolished before I was able to drink legally on licensed premises. None the less, it was an establishment in which I had some interest because I was very fond of the landlady's granddaughter who went to Parkfield Cedars, one of Derby's two girls' grammar schools. Some Monday evenings I'd meet her from her youth club in Mill Hill Lane and walk her home to Abbey Street (obviously this

The Lord Belper pub at the corner of Abbey Street and Spa Lane, pictured on a wet day in 1959.
(Author's Collection)

was several years after I'd outgrown the desire to wear obsolete military headgear). Occasionally, we'd go for a summer's afternoon walk on Darley Park. It was all wonderfully innocent and eventually, of course, it fizzled out, as these things generally do when you're in your mid-teens. Maybe she heard rumours of my past and was worried that, one day, I'd regress and turn up in a fez.

Like most streets in Derby's inner city, Abbey Street boasted several pubs. Ye Olde Spa Inne had the most interesting history, built in the eighteenth century around a mineral spring, part of a larger spa complex constructed by a man called Dr William Chauncey and actually predating Abbey Street itself. They were still brewing beer on the premises as late as 1941. Behind Ye Olde Spa stood an old building that was used as a boxing gym. On the corner of Stockbrook Street, the Pelican Inn was demolished in 1979. On the other hand, the Vine, on the corner of Wilson Street, survived until 1991 when it was closed down after the police had investigated an obscenity complaint concerning the premises. Judging by the last visit I made there, it was probably something to do with the price of its rather indifferent beer. Almost next door to the Vine, in Wilson Street, the Lifeboat was reputed to be the smallest pub in Derby. It had been around since the middle of the nineteenth century and was just a converted terrace house. On my only visit there the place was deserted and we found a bar so small that, when a couple of regulars

Ye Olde Spa Inne in the 1950s. In 2007 it was the only pub remaining in Abbey Street. (Author's Collection)

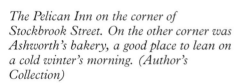

The windows of the Vine Inn get a wash. Further up Wilson Street is the Lifeboat, the smallest pub in Derby. (Author's Collection)

The Pelican Inn on the corner of Stockbrook Street. On the other corner was Ashworth's bakery, a good place to lean on a cold winter's morning. (Author's Collection)

arrived, my pal and I felt obliged to leave in order to make room for them. There'd also been an Abbey Inn, but I don't remember this; it was knocked down just before the Second World War.

Like its pubs, the other businesses in Abbey Street were varied. Opposite the Lord Belper was the butcher's shop run by Donald Sims, the man who my mother had claimed was mad. There was the Co-op cake shop, Smalley's greengrocer's, and another butcher's shop run by George Pegg. The coal yard belonged to Bill Boden, whose carthorse unconcernedly munched oats when it wasn't trotting off to deliver bags of coal, watched by wary customers like my mother. And there was Wragg's the bookies. Off-course gambling was still illegal and, in keeping with Derby's other

turf accountants, Wragg didn't advertise his business: he simply hung a
sign in the window which announced whether he was open or closed.
Violet Craven liked a bet every day. She'd write them down in pencil on
old sugar bags and ask me to take them to Wragg's, which involved
shooting a quick glance in either direction before nipping into the fog of
cigarette smoke. The whole thing was done on trust: you simply handed
over your home-made betting slip, which you'd signed with a pseudonym.
If you'd backed a winner, then you just gave your pseudonym and the
clerk would consult his ledger before paying out. I took bets in there many
times and never saw a single argument. Violet, bless her, wasn't a genius
by any means, but within seconds she could work out to the last halfpenny
how much she'd won from a ten-horse accumulator with various doubles
and trebles thrown in. 'Tell him I've got two pounds eighteen and
sixpence halfpenny to come,' she'd instruct me. I was too young to ask for
commission on her winnings; instead, payment for the errand was made
by letting me choose a bar of chocolate or some sweets from the counter
of her shop. Looking back, the chance to further my education by
sampling this nether world was probably payment enough. Eventually
Violet changed allegiance and I was sent instead to a bookie's in Wilson
Street. It was run from one of the big houses at the top of the street and
entrance was gained through the back garden. The police must have been
aware that these illegal gambling dens existed, but they were rarely raided.
Again, the scene inside the Wilson Street establishment was amazing:
dozens of men, many of them Irish labourers who lodged in the area,
listening intently to a race commentary coming over a wire service. And,
as with Wragg's, the whole room was filled with tobacco smoke which
stung the eyes and clawed at the lungs of a young non-smoker.

*Shops in Abbey
Street, looking
from the bottom of
Spa Lane.
(Author's Collection)*

But if I had to brace myself to deliver Violet's bets, then a visit to Ashworth's bakery on the corner of Stockbrook Street, opposite the Pelican, was a joyous experience. Mr Ashworth, a jolly, bespectacled individual, pulled loaves from the ovens at the back of his shop and, moments later, they were on sale. There is nothing quite so wonderful as the smell of fresh-baked bread. On snappy winter mornings it was a good idea to lean against the wall of Ashworth's bakery: the bricks were warm and you could toast your fingers. Across the road, Corden's greengrocer's shop was housed up an alleyway, not far from where my grandmother had run her tobacconist's. Ted Corden wore a brown smock, a trilby hat and sported a hook on one arm. Colin Shaw claimed that he was a retired pirate. Whether he'd ever sailed the Spanish Main I rather doubted, but he was certainly skilled at weighing out potatoes one-handed. Abbey Street Girls' School sprawled down one side of the street, next door to a fish and chip shop run by a middle-aged couple, the wife a stout woman with a London accent and plaited blonde hair. During the war, the business had been run by my mother's friends, Stan and Dolly Gregory, the Sheffield couple who'd by now taken over the Falstaff pub on Silver Hill Road in New Normanton. I'd spend many evenings in their private quarters at the Falstaff, with a pint of Iron Brew shandy (this was before the trendy spelling of recent times) and a packet of crisps, watching their television while my mother kept Stan and Dolly company in the lounge bar. The Abbey Street chip shop had a few tables and chairs in its front window for anyone who fancied what would then have passed for a night out, although I hardly ever saw them used.

Opposite the bottom of Wilson Street, Mrs Barber's wool shop was another regular port of call for my mother. I never saw her knit anything (except a black and white Derby County scarf for me, which turned out to be about 8ft long) but, again, she enjoyed the company, which seemed to be as much a shopkeeper's function as actually selling things. Next door, Davies's chemist's shop contained a surprise because Mrs Davies kept a collection of tropical fish, lizards, tree frogs and chameleons. One day she took me up to their living quarters to see this zoological delight, although no-one at school would believe me when I bragged about it afterwards. The Davies's shop stood in a row that contained William Hood's hairdresser's (Mr Hood was 'a bit of a nancy', according to my mother), Kinns the butcher (actually run by Wilf Sharman), to where my mother had taken her custom following Donald Sims's cleaver-throwing antics, and the Meadow grocery shop behind whose green-tiled frontage lay assorted biscuits in glass-topped tins, and where everything was weighed out on scales which meant much juggling of brass weights, from half an ounce to 3lb. On the other side of Alma Street, Housewives' Corner stocked pots and pans, steel wool, fire-lighters and polishes. It was a bit like Tommy Harris's but without the funny hats.

Next to the Vine, Phil Vidofsky's barber's shop was a haven for men; I was sent there every fortnight for a short back and sides and a dollop of Brylcreem. Phil was an East End Jew of Polish descent, born in the Commercial Road. His parents had moved to Derby before the First World War, to live in the Little City, a rabbit warren of narrow streets off

Corner shops like this off-licence on the corner of Stockbrook Street and Dean Street were the lifeblood of the community. (Author's Collection)

Burton Road, their names – Cannon Street, Trafalgar Street and so on – bearing testament to their origins during the Napoleonic wars. Phil's wife was also Jewish, a Cohen by birth; she was universally known as Bubby because she'd been the baby of the family. Their shop was more than just a place where hair was cut; it was a social club where, each day, the same old men would congregate – whether they needed a haircut or not – and gossip with Phil and whoever was in his chair, while Bubby kept everyone supplied with huge cups of steaming tea. I was fascinated watching Phil singe hair with lighted wax tapers, and lather men's faces before shaving them with a cut-throat razor which he kept sharp by stropping on a leather belt. My greatest day there came when I was big enough for Phil to dispense with the board that he set across the arms of the barber's chair for junior clients. When the council told Phil that his shop was in the way of Derby's planned inner ring road, he left for London. He returned five years later, opened another hairdresser's in Harry Thurman's old tobacconist's shop at the junction of Wilson Street and Gerard Street – in a direct line with his old one – ran it for twenty years, enjoyed a long retirement and eventually died at a good age, still waiting for the council to start work on that bit of the ring road. Phil's wasn't the only barber's shop in Abbey Street. His former employer, Harry Murdock, had a shop there; and it was to Arthur Waplington's shop at the bottom of Grey Street that I was sent during Phil's time back in London. Arthur was still cutting hair in Western Road, Mickleover, when he was well into his eighties.

Abbey Street certainly featured large in my formative years. Before I started school, each Thursday I'd accompany Gran Rowley to the post office there and stand with her in a queue that reeked of mothballs and Sloan's Liniment while she collected her old-age pension. The post office was run by Frank Hawley, whose premises were also home to a toy shop, which added to the attraction. If I gazed wistfully enough at some toy or other, with a bit of luck Gran might re-open her purse. One of the last businesses before Curzon Street was Alec Bennett's ironmonger's shop where you could buy two nails or a single screw, and everything came wrapped in brown paper bags rather than in inconvenient quantities hermetically sealed in plastic and cardboard. You could also buy a newspaper, a bicycle, a wireless set and a three-piece suite from this buzzing thoroughfare. You could even choose a dog or a cat from the RSPCA kennels. But whatever they sold, the businesses in Abbey Street provided more than just the tangible necessities of life. They drew their customers from the terrace houses of Gerard Street, lower Wilson Street, Grey Street and Spa Lane, from Stockbrook Street and Alma Street, houses whose front steps were scrubbed daily with something called a step-stone and whose occupants relied not on medication but on good old-fashioned over-the-counter gossip to lift their day. And probably on telling small boys that Abbey Street was a mile long, when it clearly wasn't.

CHAPTER SIX

Bemrose School . . . and a Shaving Lesson

O n the hazy morning of 6 September 1956, I stepped out towards a brave new world. Actually, that makes it sound as if I was following in the footsteps of Laurie Lee and I have to confess that mine was no epic journey on foot across the Pyrenees. All that really happened was that my father, on his way to work at the *Derby Evening Telegraph*, walked me round to 28 Crompton Street where Stuart Clay was waiting on the doorstep with his mother. Then we went down Green Lane and into Victoria Street, where my father left Stuart and me outside Ranby's store to wait for the school bus. Part of a sea of maroon caps with white hot-cross-bun piping, we boarded a green and cream Derby Corporation trolley bus which whisked us away to a new life at Bemrose School.

So it wasn't the Pyrenees, but it was still quite an adventure for an eleven-year-old boy whose previous journey to school had involved nothing more than a 100yd walk across the street. As far as I could recall, I'd never seen Bemrose, a long two-storey building with two tall towers, set in 18 acres of playing fields, until the day I stepped apprehensively up its East Drive to begin five years as a grammar school boy. There were four of us from Becket School; besides Stuart and myself, Anthony Trippett, whose father was a Spanish teacher at Bemrose, and Michael Wood had also chosen that school over Derby School. My first impression was of moving into a much more grown-up world than Becket School. To begin with some of the sixth formers appeared to be adults with their sports coats and, in one or two cases, blue-stubbled chins; and the classrooms looked more businesslike than those at Gerard Street. There were 123 new boys crowding into the main hall on that Thursday morning. Wood and Trippett, unsurprisingly, were put in the very top of the first form, with Stuart and me going into different forms lower down the pecking order. Happily, a few months later we were reunited when the school discovered that we were as daft as each other.

For the moment, however, I was on my own and I felt slightly nauseous as I trudged to my new form room, number 24, which had once been the school kitchen when the library it adjoined was the original refectory. The room overlooked the school's main entrance but it still looked like a kitchen with a half-tiled wall, two large stone sinks and several store

Bemrose School on Uttoxeter New Road. It was quite a change from Becket Juniors.
(Author's Collection)

cupboards. Then Eric 'Snoz' Branthwaite introduced himself as the man who would be our form master for the 1956-7 school year. A Yorkshiremen who sported a greying moustache and thick-rimmed spectacles, Snoz had been an English teacher at Bemrose since 1945. He had a gruff voice and, no matter what your name, he called everyone 'Willie' in a kind of growl. He made us sit in alphabetical order, so my two instant best friends were now Graham Roome from Chaddesden and Sid Smedley, a jolly-looking boy from Shakespeare Street in Sinfin. Graham already knew a boy called Mick Otton, with whom he'd gone to junior school in Chaddesden, so Sid turned round and gave me a beaming smile and a thumbs-up which meant that he and I would team up.

We were given a timetable to copy out and there then followed a tour of the school; the only thing I can still remember is the gassy smell of the chemistry labs. Afterwards we returned to Room 24 and were each given a home reader, a copy of C. Day Lewis's *The Otterbury Incident*, the story of some schoolchildren who foil a gang of criminals in postwar Britain. Snoz, although I didn't know it, was going to be a significant influence on my life. I already loved reading – books, magazines and newspapers, devouring anything I could lay my hands on – and writing essays; Snoz was an excellent English teacher, able to nurture a boy's strengths. One of his great achievements was his 'box analysis' method of breaking up the different components of a sentence. Having said all this, I found English very easy and thoroughly enjoyed it, just as other boys excelled at maths, a subject that remained a great mystery to me.

Soon it was lunchtime on that first day. I'd decided to stay for school dinners as it was too far to travel home and back, and this meant my first visit to the refectory, a long building whose walls were lined with photographs of 1st XI football and cricket teams stretching back to the 1930s. To be honest, I found the first few dinner times at Bemrose daunting. I'd never really eaten out. Our summer holidays were always spent at my grandmother's house in Spalding but, that apart, all my meals were taken at home. There were few restaurants in Derby in the 1950s, and those there were were mostly in hotels. Our family certainly never used them. So, for a while at least, I felt uncomfortable eating with strangers. Of course, my discomfort didn't last long because the strangers quickly became friends. Besides Graham and Sid, there was Mick Otton. Mick's father worked on the railway and Mick was the first person I knew who went abroad for his holidays, when Otton senior took the family to Switzerland by train. A boy called Norman Acton turned out to be a bit of a card, always getting into some scrape or other. A few days into our new adventure we were in the gymnasium at lunchtime, watching a house basketball match. Anyone entering the gym was obliged to remove their outdoor shoes. After the match was over, we emerged to find that our shoes had disappeared. Norman was the main suspect and was soon tracked down. Sure enough, the threat of having his head forced down a

Taking a break from a lunchtime game of football at Bemrose. Back row, left to right: Mick Otton, Geoff Pound, Arthur Auger, Stuart Clay and me. Front row: Peter Handford, John Cheadle, Paddy Donnelly and Barry Iremonger. (Author's Collection)

toilet was sufficient to bring him to his senses, and the hiding place for our shoes was quickly given up. My form mates were a pleasant bunch – even Norman was a nice lad, despite his penchant for always getting into mischief – and were drawn from all over Derby. Ron Midgley, Geoff Nadin and Norman Saxon (believe it or not, I later knew someone called Norman Fort) bussed in each day from Alvaston, and there was quite a crowd from Normanton, too. Tony Fry was a good soccer player, so it was ironic that, many years later, he would become one of the stalwarts of Derby Rugby Club.

Ian Foster's father ran a butcher's shop near the Cavendish; Ian Brownson's mother had gone to school with mine; Peter Malkin lived in the Firs Estate area, off Boyer Street, and always seemed to be smiling; Allen Blanchard was another smiler, a bespectacled lad who seemed to be in a perpetually good mood. John Godfrey seemed to have been bitten by a religious bug and kept quoting from the Bible (he later became a Labour councillor in Derby); David Garry Fretwell Smith (few of us had three first names) was a large lad who was instantly dubbed 'Bopper' after The Big Bopper, the pop singer who, three years later, was to perish in the plane crash which also claimed the lives of Buddy Holly and Ritchie Valens. Andrew Birley wasn't keen on games, but then he didn't want to be a professional footballer and fifty years later Dr Andrew Birley would e-mail me from Australia to say that he was retiring from the Genetic Epidemiology Group at the Queensland Institute of Medical Research in Brisbane. Pearse Kennedy was one of the few Roman Catholic boys at Bemrose: the RCs would hold a separate daily assembly, taken by a white-haired classics teacher, 'Killer' Blake, a Dublin University graduate who, despite his nickname, displayed a leprechaun humour.

Although we didn't find ourselves in the same form until the following year, one lad from Newlyn Drive, off Village Street in Normanton, was to become a lifelong friend. I was already aware of John Cheadle because he played in our Newton House football team, a cheeky little centre-forward with a good turn of speed and a strong shot; he was also a very good tennis player and a decent medium-pace bowler who always seemed to drop on a length from the first ball of the season. On the face of it we were unlikely pals: I was quite tall for my age (I started shaving when I was barely fourteen) and looked a lot older than my years; John, meanwhile, was a little lad with a fresh face who looked much younger than he was. The irony was that, although he was actually three months older than me, he was the one who later stopped us getting into Certificate X films. Cinema managers would always let me through but they always put the block on John. In the end, we'd go for a game of snooker. In fact, that was our usual routine. We played at the Regent billiard hall in Babington Lane, where there were twenty-four tables, each rented out at 2s an hour. Rather than risk running up a bill we couldn't afford, we'd pay up front and then hope that Mrs Day, who seemed to run the place, hadn't noticed. Many's the time the light would be switched off and, with only the pink and black to pot, we'd play on in the gloom until we'd finished the game or got kicked off the table, whichever came first. Then we'd repair to the Becket Well Café in Macklin Street or the

Wardwick Milk Bar, where I'd have a Horlicks; John's favourite tipple was a banana milk-shake. When we left school, he went to work at the Co-op travel department, where the manager was Arthur Hill, in his younger days a well-known runner with Derby and County Athletic Club. John later signed up with Stuart Webb, the Derby County secretary who had just purchased a travel company. Together they built it up into one of the biggest in the UK and John began taking top football clubs, and even the England team, all over Europe, his banana milk-shake days well and truly behind him.

One day, I was playing in a form football match when I recognised the fenland drawl of a new boy on the opposing side. Arthur Auger (Terence Arthur Auger actually but we already had a Terry – King) had come to Bemrose from Wisbech Grammar School in Cambridgeshire; his father had obtained a job at Rolls-Royce. Arthur shouldn't even have been at secondary school in Derby as he was born one month after the start of the school year here. In Cambridgeshire, however, the school year started a full month earlier and, as he'd already been at grammar school for twelve months, it seemed daft to push him back to the first form. Arthur, who joined our form shortly after we'd first met, was a larger than life character in more ways than one with a round, beaming face and a loud, raucous laugh. But it was an incident at the start of the 1958 summer term that cemented his reputation. In Wisbech in the summer months it was the custom to spend the hours immediately after school helping on the land and thus khaki shorts were *de rigueur* from May until July. Quite why Arthur hadn't noticed that inner-city Derby wasn't exactly over-blessed with farmyards and fields full of crops to tend I don't know, but he caused an uproar on the first day of the new term by turning up in a pair of voluminous khaki shorts of the kind normally seen only in a Morecambe and Wise sketch. There was apparently some debate among the teachers as to whether he should be sent home immediately to change into the regulation long grey flannel trousers worn by the rest of us. In the end it was decided that he could remain in lessons and remedy his sartorial *faux pas* the following day. It certainly amused us, and probably the teachers too, but Arthur had too well-rounded a personality to let it bother him and he enjoyed the joke as much as anyone. He and I became close friends.

Along with another good pal, Terry King, we played cricket for Derby Red Rose, a club based at the railway where Terry's father, Harry, worked. Both sets of parents, the Augers and the Kings, and indeed the Cheadles, welcomed me into their homes with open arms and this was a very happy time in my life. When we left school, Arthur and Terry joined the RAF and before they went their separate ways they were based at Halton in Buckinghamshire, where we took a football team down to play against their intake. In 1976, his military service over, Arthur took a job with British Aerospace in Saudi Arabia. One night a couple of years later, I was idly watching *News at Ten* on ITV when Arthur's picture suddenly flashed up on the screen. I put down the newspaper I was half-reading and listened intently as Reginald Bosanquet told the nation that my mate Arthur, together with a chap called Derek Raines, had been arrested in

Saudi Arabia after being caught working the biggest illegal still ever built in the kingdom. They had each been sentenced to three years in prison and 300 lashes. I rang Arthur's parents and over the next few months guided them through the media storm that inevitably broke over the family. Arthur did about a year in prison and received his lashes before being released. Of course he made light of it all, just as he had his khaki shorts all those years earlier. A free man once more, Arthur bought a general provisions store in Castle Donington and also began an outside catering business for which he showed considerable flair. Alas, his enthusiasm sometimes ran away with him and he ended up working in a number of clubs and pubs, in Derby and then in the West Midlands. The last time I saw him he was waiting to draw his RAF pension, whereupon he was going to buy a camper van and emigrate to Bulgaria 'where I can live like a millionaire on thirty quid a week'.

Looking back to my first days at Bemrose School, it was inevitable that Poupee Gupta would stand out from the crowd in the autumn of 1956. Of the 768 boys on the roll at the start of that school year, his was the only non-white face. Poupee had arrived in England in 1950, from Calcutta, to join his father who was working in London as an ear, nose and throat surgeon. Eventually, the family moved to Nottingham, then to Derby where Gupta senior took a post at the Derbyshire Royal Infirmary. The family lodged on Kedleston Road, ironically, and sometimes awkwardly, the paying guests of a hospital porter who also worked at the DRI. Poupee went first to St Philomena's Convent School, then to Ashgate School, on Ashbourne Road, before, on that September morning over fifty years ago, walking hesitantly through the east gate at Bemrose. In 1958, Poupee and his family returned to Calcutta, and, over the years, I'd often wondered what happened to the gentle little Indian boy with the impeccable manners, whose enthusiasm for football (his loyalty was divided between the Rams and Stanley Matthews) knew no bounds. Nor, for that matter, did his sheer delight at simply being at Bemrose, where the house system, a Latin motto, and masters wearing gowns, all fitted perfectly with the images he'd formed while reading the classic schoolboy fiction of Frank Richards and Thomas Hughes. Thanks to Poupee's own book, *Salaam Stanley Matthews*, I eventually found the answer. His proper name is Subrata Dasgupta (Poupee is a childhood nickname) and after going to university in India and Canada, he became director of cognitive science, an eminent chair in computer science, and professor of history at the University of Louisiana in the USA. So Poupee did rather better than most of us, but he's apparently never forgotten his days as a Derby schoolboy, which says a lot for the school and the town, as it then was.

A boy whose whereabouts I initially lost touch with was Brian Staley, who eventually became our local milkman. Brian was another nice lad, an uncomplicated character who, for one year, sat next to me in Room 24 as the alphabetical list of pupils turned from one row of desks into another. Like me, Brian was good at English and bad at maths, so there was no point in us cribbing off each other. He was also a good artist whose main speciality was drawing horses. In fact, Brian could almost always be caught doodling a horse's head, which earned him the universal nickname of 'Dobbin'. He lived at Mackworth and could be seen each lunchtime, hurtling back home on his bike, even before the rest of us had gathered our books together. His father was a milkman and Brian eventually took on the round. He and his wife also became foster parents to dozens of Derby youngsters fortunate enough to have found such a caring family. Terry King also had a talent for drawing, although his only party piece was Andy Capp, the chauvinistic cartoon character who appeared in the *Daily Mirror*. Much to the annoyance of the teachers, Kingy's exercise books were heavily decorated with representations of Andy and his missus, the long-suffering Flo.

Two lads who were almost inseparable were Barry Iremonger and David Donnelly. The latter was always known as Paddy because, despite his broad Derby accent, he was Irish. His father owned quite a bit of property in Hartington Street, a once-genteel thoroughfare off Normanton Road (so posh, in fact, that in the early years of the twentieth century, the street was gated at both ends to prevent the riff-raff from using it as a short cut). Paddy himself was an Ulsterman, born in the Tyrone township of Cookstown before his family moved to England after the war. The one thing I can remember about Paddy is that he was always laughing; absolutely everything amused him. Ten minutes in his company and you were usually crying with laughter yourself, although not quite sure why. Barry Iremonger was also popular, not least because he lived in a pub. His father had been killed in a railway accident, and Barry and his mother lived with her parents who kept the Crescent Vaults on the corner of Shaftesbury Crescent and Malcolm Street, close to the Baseball Ground. Because of his late father's job, Barry qualified for free or quarter-fare rail travel, which he would share with us. It came in useful when we were travelling all over England to watch Derby County. He and I once went to see the Rams play at Charlton Athletic. Imagine it: two fourteen-year-old boys going all the way to London, changing at Blackheath, watching the match, calling at Leicester Square for egg and chips on the way back, then arriving at Derby station after midnight and walking home. It's an adventure that few parents would allow today. Yet, half a century ago, no-one batted an eyelid and we felt perfectly safe.

Alan Thompson was another quiet lad. His father had been working on the East African Railways but had returned temporarily to Derby, so Alan joined us at Bemrose. He was a keen footballer and came with us to watch Derby County; once we travelled all the way to Brighton for an FA Cup match. In the autumn of 1961 I received a letter from Alan, who had returned to Tanganyika with his family. It was full of memories of our days watching the Rams, and of his news, playing football on a rough pitch with bushes for touchlines and the game constantly interrupted by people with piles of washing on their head, taking a short cut across the playing area. 'We'll be coming home soon', wrote Alan, 'now that the Africans have taken over.' He said that they would be sailing back to Britain on the SS *Braemar Castle*. Sadly, I never heard from him again. Another boy with whom I chummed up but who mysteriously disappeared was Geoff Parsons, who had arrived from Swindon to live at the St Christopher's Railway Orphanage on Ashbourne Road. One teatime we'd walked down the school drive and were saying cheerio at the top of Uttoxeter Old Road when Geoff said, 'I might not see you again. I can't explain. Just some bother at St Christopher's.' He was right: he didn't turn up for school the next day and I never did see him again, which was a great shame because he was a terrific lad and a good footballer. I assumed a girl was involved.

And, of course, there was Stuart Clay, my pal from our Becket School days. Stuart's father, Teddy, was a Labour member of Derby Borough Council and chairman of the Watch Committee which administered Derby's borough police force. He was also an undertaker with the Co-op, which was a source of amusement to Stuart's schoolmates ('Is it true your dad's got a dead-end job?' or 'Is he on the skeleton staff?'). The Clay family – Stuart had an older brother and sister – lived in a big house just around the corner from the Hippodrome Theatre in Green Lane. Like many of the large houses in the area, they took in 'theatricals' and Teddy was always going on about Frankie Howerd: 'Dirty bugger stopped here for a week and never changed his shirt once.' One week, a comedy duo called Morecambe and Wise stayed at the Clays; one afternoon, Eric and Ernie took Stuart, his brother, Richard, and his sister, Gladys, to the fair on Bass's Rec. That must have been quite an experience, although Morecambe and Wise, albeit quite well known, hadn't achieved the fame that later came their way with those legendary television shows in the 1970s. Stuart joined Derby Borough police in 1961 and retired thirty-four years later, still a constable happy to pound the beat in Derby.

So, the boys of Bemrose Grammar School were drawn from all over the town, even deep into the county: Malcolm Spare, who, like Stuart Clay, joined the police force, travelled in each day from Melbourne, a small, attractive Georgian market town near the Leicestershire border. They were also a varied crew: the sons of surgeons and spot welders, pathologists and printers. However, none were quite so exotic, to our eyes at least, as Dave Budzinski and Whiff Spiers. One morning, as form captain, I was called out of a chemistry lesson and told to go to Dr Chapman's study. I'd never been inside the headmaster's den before, and racked my brain trying to recall what I'd done wrong. Waiting inside with Doc Chapman were two American boys whose fathers had come over to Derby for a year to work at Rolls-Royce, bringing their families with them. Whiff Spiers sported a crew-cut and a pronounced limp, the result either of a childhood accident or polio, I can't remember which. Dave Budzinski had wavy hair and wore thick-rimmed spectacles. Both were put in my house, Newton, and then I was told to take them back to the chemistry lab and introduce them to the rest of the form. The teacher, Maurice Dunthorne, promptly suspended the lesson and allowed a question-and-answer session. This was when I became aware of the old saying, 'Two nations divided by a common language.' What they called erasers, we called rubbers – which was what they called condoms. So to ask them for a rubber brought the house down. But not so much as when Arthur Auger told one of them, 'I'll be back in a jiffy.' Jiffy was apparently the name of a brand of American condom. They were grand lads and fitted in well. One raw February night, I took them to the Baseball Ground to see their first-ever game of soccer. I think it was probably also their last. They were frozen, Derby lost to Charlton Athletic, and, like most of the 15,000 crowd that night, Dave and Whiff went home disillusioned.

With or without its American influence (Dave Budzinski was a decent sprinter), Newton House turned out to be the Manchester United of the Bemrose house system, sweeping almost everything before them. Obviously this was largely down to the luck of the draw with Newton having enjoyed all the best footballers, cricketers, athletes and swimmers of each new intake over the previous five years. It was also due, however, to a sixth-former called Bob Wilson (his twin brother, Bill, was also at the school) who seemed to inspire the best in most people (not me, though; he once told me how disappointed he was that I'd skived off the house cross-country championship because of an alleged heavy cold). Bob Wilson was one of those irritating youths who was good at everything. Football, cricket, athletics, music, drama – he was into everything with a vengeance. I bet if they'd entered him for the Grand National and the Boat Race as well, he would have jumped at the chance. Newton also had a rather sweet housemaster, a history teacher called William Norville, whose nickname was 'Nunky' or sometimes 'Humble' on account of his demeanour. He cared about his boys, though, and once devoted an entire history lesson to the art of shaving, which I found rather tedious since I'd been scraping off my whiskers for a year or more.

Throughout my years at Bemrose, I always enjoyed morning assembly when the entire school, masters and pupils, would congregate in the main hall at 9 a.m. Every morning, except Fridays when we had house prayers, we sang a couple of hymns from *Hymns Ancient and Modern* to the accompaniment of the magnificent school organ (played in my early days at Bemrose by a music teacher, Kenneth Eade, who was also the organist at St Werburgh's Church) and the school choir, who sat in the organ gallery. Prayers were said and school notices read out by the duty house master (on Mondays this included the previous Saturday's sports results), all presided over by the headmaster, complete in his gown and mortarboard. The assembly brought everyone together and gave us a daily reminder that we were a family. It also helped me to learn the words of some of the country's finest hymns and appreciate the wonderful language of those Victorian hymn writers.

My first year at grammar school was bewildering enough, getting to grips with new surroundings, new faces, new rules and regulations, but I was also acutely aware of events in the wider world. As the last few days of the unseasonably cool August of 1956 slipped away, I'd devoured every bit of news concerning the crisis unfolding in the Middle East, where the Egyptian president, Colonel Nasser, had recently nationalised the Suez Canal. My father was firmly on the side of the Prime Minister, Sir Anthony Eden, who wanted to march into Egypt and get it back again, and over the next few weeks the crisis gathered pace with an Anglo-French airborne invasion of the Canal Zone and then a rollicking from President Eisenhower which meant that, in November, the British and French had to withdraw. 'Bloody Yanks', muttered my father, without looking up from his *Daily Mail*. 'They've always been the bloody same.'

By now, however, another international crisis, nearer to home, had my attention. In a response to a national uprising led by Prime Minister Imre Nagy, who has promised the Hungarian people independence and political freedom, the Soviet Union had invaded Hungary. One early November teatime, on my way to the corner shop, I bumped into Colin Shaw. 'Have you seen the news?' he asked. 'Ferenc Puskas has been killed.' Puskas had played in the Hungary soccer side that had beaten England 6–3 at Wembley three years earlier. According to the English sporting press, he was short, stocky, barrel-chested, overweight, couldn't head and used only one foot. But he was a brilliant inside-forward, known as the 'Galloping Major' because he was, technically at least, an army officer (his club, Honved, was a state-sponsored army team). Now, apparently, he'd been killed in the bitter street fighting that raged in the Hungarian capital, Budapest. I was shocked. I'd seen him only in flickering black and white television pictures, but the thought that he'd been killed fighting the Russians occupied me for several days. It eventually turned out that Puskas and the rest of the Honved team had actually been on tour at the time of the Soviet invasion, so he did the sensible thing and, instead of returning home, went to Spain instead and became a footballing legend with Real Madrid. I made a note to double-check anything that Colin Shaw told me in future.

The Soviet invasion of Hungary soon had an impact locally as well. Donington Hall, just over the border in Leicestershire but only a few miles from Derby (one day it would become the headquarters of British Midland Airways), had been converted into a reception centre for refugees from the fighting. Soon there were complaints that displaced Hungarians had turned the Hall into a rubbish tip. Then a letter, written under the pseudonym 'Chaddesden', appeared in the *Derby Evening Telegraph*: 'No matter how many people of other nationalities seek refuge in this country, they always thrive at the expense of our own people.' Some viewpoints never change.

The main thing that occurred to me, however, was that with the Russians invading parts of Eastern Europe, and apparently also sticking their noses into the Suez business, what had become known as the Cold War was developing into a real threat. The constant image of Russian tanks pointing menacingly towards Western Europe began to focus my mind on the eventual probability of National Service. After all, every July sixth-formers were leaving Bemrose and being conscripted before they could carry on to university. Schoolboys one day were becoming soldiers the next. It would still be four or five years before that happened to me, but the troubling thought was there. One day I was browsing through the shelves at the public library in the Wardwick when I spotted a booklet entitled something like *National Service: Your Options*. I thought I'd better take some notes. I soon discovered that, with an O-Level in English Language, once you'd done your basic training you could apply to become an instant sergeant in the Royal Army Education Corps. Spending two years teaching illiterate conscripts how to read and write sounded a much better idea than facing the Russians on the North German Plain, or hacking your way through the Malayan jungle. I took down some details and put them away until the dreadful day dawned. Of course, it never did. By the time the very last National Servicemen left the Army, I'd been at work for two years, the final intakes having been determined by the lottery of birth dates. Many of my contemporaries have said that they are sorry they missed National Service; personally, I was just mightily relieved.

In the summer of 1957, we paid 10s each for a first-form day out to London by train, the highlights of which were to be a boat trip down the Thames as far as Greenwich, then a bus trip out to London Airport at Heathrow. I found the river trip interesting enough as our little boat picked its way between snorting tugs and barges, while steamships unloaded their cargoes alongside the warehouses at bustling docks with names like Surrey Commercial, West India, East India and Millwall. However, the trip out to London Airport was, in my opinion at least, a complete waste of time. We were driven around without being allowed to get out of the bus and my overriding impression was of a lot of grass and, about a mile away, the smudge of a control tower. Some lads on the back seats got very excited because they claimed to have seen a Bristol Brabazon airliner parked on a runway, but since my later investigations showed that only one Brabazon was ever built, and that had been scrapped four years before we got to Heathrow, I assume they must have been overwhelmed by the sheer excitement of leaving Derby for the day. Personally, I found the escapologist on Tower Green much more entertaining, and, in retrospect, I'm glad that I was able to listen to the great pacifist orator, Donald Soper, addressing a crowd nearby. Both were far more illuminating than a long-distance view of an airport control tower, and far more enjoyable than the rubbery meal of poached egg on toast that we were later presented with at St Pancras station, in a large, dusty dining room that looked as if it had last been used to accommodate travellers on their way to the coronation of Edward VII.

My main problem at grammar school was that, to my continued embarrassment, I looked several years older than I really was (when I was in the fourth form, I was once reprimanded for having stubble) and yet until I was almost sixteen, along with everyone else I was supposed to wear the regulation school cap which already sat uneasily on the head of even the smallest fresh-faced boy. It was a rule that everyone up to and including the fourth form had to wear the cap to and from school. It was a nonsense that, while I could easily have called in for a pint and no one would have guessed that I was still some way short of the legal drinking age, at the same time I was given a detention by a physics master called Les Manchester, who spotted me one teatime walking home minus my cap; I was only a couple of hundred yards from our house, but I still had to serve the detention. It was these silly rules that prevented me from throwing myself wholeheartedly into life at Bemrose in the way that many other boys did. I never, for instance, joined any of the clubs or societies that proliferated. There was never any likelihood that I would sign up for the Scientific Society (the title of one lecture alone, Homogeneous Co-ordinates, was enough to daunt me), the Christian Union (which on one occasion was bizarrely teamed up with the Gramophone Society for an address by the headmaster) or the Chess Club. The United Nations Society attracted regular attendances of 100 or more, but it was not for me. And I was far too unsure of myself to sally forth into the Debating Society. That only left the Music, Arts and Crafts clubs, and I had no talent for any of those disciplines. I also found myself railing against the house system, probably because of its obsession with cross country running. We were often called back after school to go running, and whenever it rained on a games day it seemed that the school couldn't declare the football pitches unfit quick enough, and instead sent everyone running around the school playing field – all 18 acres of it – and then up the steep Rykneld Rec hill, around the ring road and back again. It was at the top of Rykneld Rec hill that I was spectacularly sick after being forced to undertake a cross country run not long after I'd enjoyed two helpings of treacle pudding and custard on the second sitting for school dinner. Cross country running seemed as pointless as learning algebra.

Thankfully, there seemed very little bullying at Bemrose, although I would probably have escaped most of it, being quite tall and looking older than I was. True, there was an initiation that almost every new pupil had to go through: being thrown into a large holly bush on the East Drive. And you would occasionally be standing at a urinal when a group of boys would charge in and clamp some unfortunate's hands to a copper hot-water pipe that ran along the outer wall (it sounds dreadful but the water wasn't all that hot and the whole thing was more of a gesture against someone who'd got too big for their boots). But I never saw any gratuitous bullying. The nearest to a victim in our form was a small boy called Ronnie Mears, whose trousers were continually being hidden during PE lessons, thus obliging Mears to enter the next class in his football shorts. One particular session of PE was immediately followed by a maths lesson taken by Pongo Molyneux. Every week the scene was the same. We'd be just be under way when the door would creak open and there would stand the forlorn figure of little Ronnie, smartly dressed in regulation blazer, shirt, tie, socks, highly-polished black shoes – and football shorts. We all knew what was coming next. Pongo would stare at Ronnie for a moment and then ask wearily, 'Who has Mears's trousers this week?' Then he would take Ronnie by the ear and lead him into the middle of the classroom: 'You miserable boy . . . why don't you ever look after your trousers?' Ronnie would begin to protest, Pongo would release him with an exasperated 'Oh, go and sit down', and at the end of the lesson, the poor lad would be reunited with his bags once more. I last saw Ronnie in about 1963, trying to control a Corporation lawnmower on the central reservation of Bradshaw Way. He wasn't wearing football shorts, so I like to think he wasn't permanently scarred by the experience.

Like my fellow pupils, the teachers at Bemrose also proved to be a very mixed bunch, and there was none more colourful than Herbert Cook who, for four years, attempted to teach us French. He was the most eccentric and amusing teacher any of us had ever encountered. Herbert, a Yorkshireman, was a Sheffield United fanatic who would spend half the lesson extolling the virtues of the Blades before realising that he hadn't broached the subject he was supposed to be teaching. Then he'd simply

Christmas 1959 and Herbert Cook is in a jolly mood, so someone takes his photograph. Pupils left to right are me, Mick Otton, Peter Malkin and Terry King's nose. (Author's Collection)

say, 'You lot think you've got me talking but, believe me, this is far more important than learning French grammar.' He was a brilliant linguist who spoke fluent French, German, Italian and Flemish, as well as several obscure dialects of those languages. In his French class we used a textbook that he'd written. He was a funny looking character with a shock of ginger hair, an almost corpse-like complexion and a lean frame. He chain-smoked, wore two pullovers (the outer one normally had a large hole) over which he pulled his underpants, and a sports coat under his chalk-covered gown. He was a great jazz fan and one day came into the form room, put a new thorn (not a needle) in his gramophone, set a 78rpm record playing, and then just sat back and stared out of the window. On another occasion we arrived for a French lesson to find the second half of England v. Spain at Wembley just getting under way on his ancient wireless set. 'Not a word!' he roared, and we just sat there and listened to the rest of the match. Herbert had a special way of marking exercise books. Your work would come back with the mistakes circled many times in brilliant red ink, marks of minus five, and words like 'Dolt!', 'Oaf!', 'Buffoon!' or 'Cor!!!' scrawled in the margins.

He was both our French teacher and our form master in Room 42, at the top of the west stairs, where a special bond developed between teacher and pupils. It was based on healthy competition, a respectful sparring between man and boys. One day, someone left a boot print on the freshly painted ceiling of our form room. Herbert reeled back in horror before exclaiming, 'Forensic science will out the perpetrator.' Then he called me to the front of the class (I was that year's form captain) and together we began to examine the soles of everyone's shoes. One by one, my fellow pupils were made to come out and lift up their left foot. Of course, whoever had done the deed simply swapped shoes with someone else, so somewhere along the way Herbert and I inspected the same footwear twice. When everyone had been seen, he slumped back in his chair. He looked so bewildered that I felt sorry for him. Then he just sighed, 'As I thought, it must have been an intruder', and we all carried on as though none of this pantomime had happened. Sometimes he would tell a boy that he was 'enough to curdle my Weetabix', or he would suddenly announce in the middle of a lesson that there was 'a fortune awaiting the chap who introduces chip pans into Western Germany'.

Where many teachers would hand out pointless punishments like lines, those Herbert meted out were always constructive. Once he caught me daydreaming. When I finally realised that he was talking to me and responded, he ordered me to write a 500-word essay on delayed-action bombs, which meant a fair bit of research. Bemrose also had a system of detentions which involved being kept behind on Thursday teatimes for such offences as handing in homework late. Herbert would hand these out like confetti – 'Right, you've got a Thursday', he'd warble – but he never actually logged them into the system, so they became meaningless. We began a league table which we pinned to the form notice board. One day he asked what it was and we told him, whereupon everyone on the list was given an official detention and they duly had to serve it. There was plenty of room for banter and jousting, but we had to remember who was ultimately in control.

A measure of Herbert Cook's wit and memory can be gauged from an incident concerning dinner money. Every Monday morning, I had to help him count the cash collected from those staying to dinners that week, and then I would take the money to the school secretary. The cost of school dinners had just gone up from 9d to 1s, and one Monday morning, when we came to tot it up, we were 6d over. Fast forward thirty years to Derby public library in the Wardwick. I was bending down to take a book off a shelf when I was aware of someone standing over me. I looked up and it was Herbert Cook, still looking much the same as the last time I'd seen him three decades earlier. 'Hello Rippon', he said, 'I was only thinking of you the other day. We never did solve that mystery of the phantom half a dinner, did we?' Three decades had elapsed but that little incident was how he remembered me. Before I could answer, he was gone. I was sad to read of Herbert's death a few years later. Sadder still to see that he'd instructed that his funeral service was to be strictly private with no mourners other than his immediate family. I believe the crematorium would have been full of his former pupils wanting to pay their last respects.

If I was never the brightest pupil when it came to learning French, maths left me totally bewildered. I could manage arithmetic, not least because every primary school pupil arrived at their secondary school well prepared for long division and multiplication (the learning by rote of the times table help enormously here). But I was utterly useless at algebra, probably because I could never see the point in bothering to learn it unless you intended to pursue a career building atomic bombs. Geometry was slightly more useful, if you wanted to work out how many square yards of carpet you needed, or how much paint for the walls – but algebra? Fortunately, my ineptitude for the subject was quickly recognised by our maths master, Roger Molyneux, known to everyone as Pongo. There were two myths about Pongo: that he was a Liverpudlian and that his nervous facial tic was due to shell shock suffered in the First World War. He was actually born in Derby, in 1909. He could have grown up on Merseyside, of course, but he would have been only nine years old when that terrible war ended. There were also rumours of his left-wing leanings and this I can vouch for: Pongo lived near me in the 1980s and we'd often have a forthright debate about politics; he was certainly no lover of Margaret Thatcher. Like many of his profession, he possessed an unerring aim with a board rubber or a piece of chalk. Less usual, he had a habit of gently rubbing his nose with his tie; often he would look up to see his entire form doing the same. Pongo understood me and never put any pressure on me to tackle complicated algebraic equations (he probably realised that he'd just be wasting his time). Instead, he'd send me out in the middle of a lesson to buy his pipe tobacco. As long as he felt that I was usefully employed, he seemed happy enough. He once wrote on my maths report, 'A long illness, patiently borne', so he was something of a comedian as well.

Pongo Molyneux and Herbert Cook were two teachers who made a huge impact on me without actually teaching me very much. The splendidly named Oliver George Donald Goldfinch taught me a great deal. Olly came from to Bemrose in 1960 from Emanuel School, London. He taught English and also waxed lyrically about his beloved Charlton Athletic. He picked me out as his star pupil and told me which books to read and how to become a better writer. In the late 1990s I tracked him down to Droitwich Spa, to where he had retired, and we exchanged correspondence for a while. It was all general stuff about Bemrose School in his day, and I'm not sure that he actually remembered me, but I certainly remembered him, a fact that seemed to please him. Everyone remembered Danny Rees, the fierce Welsh PE teacher with the tattered black tracksuit. Danny, who had served in the RAF during the Second World War, was a fine rugby player, a regular for Derby Tigers RFC. He also had a quick temper which spelled trouble in those less enlightened days when it was perfectly acceptable for teachers to thump their pupils whenever they felt like it (although, for some strange reason, caning had to be properly administered with an entry in the Bemrose punishment book). There were two ways in which you could suffer at the hands of Danny Rees. There were the summary public beatings when someone had annoyed him, perhaps by chewing gum. And then there was the premeditated stuff, the more considered invitation to his room after school. This was a tiny office next to the gymnasium, where he would bounce errant pupils off the walls. I was told to go there only once, and I was fortunate to arrive just as he was about to referee an important house basketball match. He pondered for a moment, wondering whether he had time to thump me a few times and still make the basketball tip-off. Happily, time was pressing and so he threw me a tin of dubbin, a large cloth, and pointed towards a pile of footballs. When I'd spent half an hour dubbining the balls, then I could go. It was finger-aching but nowhere near as bad as the alternative. Fifteen years after I'd left Bemrose, I returned to play cricket against the staff team. Danny was still turning out and afterwards we enjoyed a few pints together in the nearby Bedford Arms. He had apparently just recovered from a nervous breakdown. I imagine it was because the government had changed the rules on beating up pupils. He probably felt unfulfilled.

For our second year, we said goodbye to Snoz as our form master, although he still taught us English, and moved upstairs, where we came under the wing of a history teacher called Dick Cannon. In the 1950s, Dick seemed to have leapt straight from the pages of a P.G. Wodehouse novel and time certainly didn't change him. In the summer of 1975 I was returning from a holiday in Bournemouth when, to my amazement, Dick Cannon boarded our train at Reading. He was wearing a straw boater, a multi-coloured striped blazer, and appeared to be in charge of a group of boys from a minor boarding school. He became embroiled in an argument with the ticket inspector about the non-appearance of the seats he'd apparently reserved. There was a lot of finger-wagging as Dick gave the inspector a piece of his mind. I watched in fascination, marvelling at the fact that this comical figure from my boyhood had briefly reappeared in my life. The inspector decided he'd had enough and walked off. My last sighting of Dick Cannon was of him pursuing his quarry out of the carriage, still wagging his finger and threatening to write to the Minister of Transport about the whole disgraceful affair.

When I first arrived at Bemrose, the headmaster was Eric Bennett, a hawkish-looking man with a steely gaze and no discernible sense of humour. He had been at Bemrose since 1951, although he was no stranger to Derby, having been an assistant languages master at Derby School after leaving Downing College, Cambridge, in 1932. During the Second World War, he'd served with the Intelligence Corps in Italy and Austria, and had been mentioned in despatches before being demobbed in 1946 with the rank of major. He was a remote figure in many ways, but one day he took our English class and seemed to single me out as a promising student, in that subject at least. Bennett had a thing about television. He once told a school speech day that he'd been horrified to learn that in one of the fifth forms, half the pupils admitted to watching television for 1½ hours each evening. He conceded that some of the programmes might have had some educational value but, by and large, regarded television as a 'supine affair'. He was delighted to learn that my family didn't own a TV set.

Five Bemrose staff who left after my first year. From left to right: Dick Smith tried to teach me French; Bill Spencer gave a bewildering sex education lesson; John Carter was a First World War hero; headmaster Eric Bennett was pleased that we didn't own a TV; music master Bill Eade told me that I couldn't sing. (Derby Evening Telegraph)

After my first year, Eric Bennett left to become headmaster of a school in Bournemouth and he was eventually replaced by Dr W.R.C. Chapman. Like Mr Bennett, Dr Chapman wore both gown and mortarboard; unlike his predecessor, he always wore the broadest smile. Like Bennett, though, he also had a distinguished war record, serving as a flight lieutenant in RAF intelligence and working at Bletchley Park, where, as a brilliant linguist, his job was to make sense of the often garbled German unscrambled from the Enigma Code machine. Before the Battle of El Alamein, he had been sent to Egypt and put in charge of a listening post, sending back intelligence to Bletchley Park, for which he was also mentioned in despatches. Of course, the young schoolboys in his charge at Bemrose knew nothing of this (even if he'd felt like boasting, which would have been extremely unlikely, for years after the war he was also bound by the Official Secrets Act). Ray Chapman, as he liked to be known to his friends, never said one word to me during the three years we were both at Bemrose. But in 1995 I was speaking to Derby Rotary Club, of which he was a member, when he came up, shook hands, and said he'd been so looking forward to seeing me again. Whether he really remembered me, or whether he was just being polite, I will never know. Either way, it was a nice gesture.

There were at least two other Bemrose masters who could look back on fine war records. The deputy headmaster, the silver-haired John Carter, had been awarded the Military Cross while serving in the Machine Gun Company in Salonika in 1918. Bill Smellie, who taught Latin and Greek, had also won the Military Cross, in his case for rushing an enemy machine-gun post in Gallipoli in 1915, while serving with the Royal Scots Fusiliers. Reading their *London Gazette* citations after all these years is a humbling experience. But fifty years ago, how could we have known, as we sat listening to Bill Smellie tell us that 'the Phoenicians had a good supply of food on the hoof', that he was such a hero, a man who charged enemy machine-gun posts? There had also been heroes among the pupils: the roll of honour in the school library paid testament to that. Headed *Lux Perpetua Luceat Eis* (Let perpetual light shine on them), the board listed almost ninety Old Bemrosians who had lost their lives in the Second World War. I often used to look at it and wonder at their stories which were told, in the briefest detail, in a book which also carried their photographs, earnest young men looking awkward in military uniform. They included John Banks, at Bemrose from 1932 to 1935, killed in action in Normandy in 1944 and buried at Bayeux; Harold Granger, who left Bemrose in 1935, joined the RAF and died in a Japanese prisoner-of-war camp a few months before the war in the Far East ended; Bill Poxon, at Bemrose from 1933 to 1937, who was lost when the *Prince of Wales* was sunk off Malaya in December 1941; Maurice Lee of the Sherwood Foresters, who was killed in a Jewish terrorist outrage in Palestine in 1947. Lest we forget.

On a lighter note, there was another reminder of the Second World War at Bemrose School in the 1950s. The more practical subjects were taught down on Albany Road, in a former Air Raid Precautions centre that had been hastily erected in the dark days of 1939. Getting there involved crossing the busy main road to Uttoxeter. Amazingly, so far as I know, no one was ever hit by a car, despite the fact that a proper pedestrian crossing wasn't installed until the late 1990s, by which time the ARP centre had been knocked down and houses built in its place, so there was no need for Bemrose pupils to cross the road there anyway. As I was absolutely useless at woodwork and metalwork, the periods spent at Albany Road were a complete nightmare, a fact not helped by two of the teachers.

Ronnie Hanlon, the woodwork master, a small man with a spinal deformity, was himself a former Bemrose pupil who'd returned in 1940 to teach at the school, five years later surprising everyone by marrying a tall,

Mick Otton and me at the frightful handicraft centre situated in a Second World War ARP centre on Albany Road. (Author's Collection)

attractive woman who taught biology. Ronnie struck fear into new boys with a stern lecture on road safety – 'They had to scraaaape him off the road' – and part of his welcoming speech involved cracking a lathe strap across his desk to produce an ear-shattering thunderclap that had nervous first-formers quaking in their new shoes. Ronnie was one of the most dangerous teachers in the school. He had a deskful of offensive weapons, could throw lumps of wood and chisels with unerring accuracy, and had a favourite habit of fastening a boy's tie (he was still wearing it, of course) into a desk vice and leaving the errant pupil there for the remainder of the lesson. Yet Ronnie appreciated pupils who tried hard, whatever their ability, and was well liked by those he trusted. In fact, behind the frightening exterior lay a gentle, sensitive man with a deep, educated voice. I believe he was a good pianist; certainly, he once led our Newton House to first place in a music competition.

This is more than could be said for his metalwork counterpart, Bill 'Boney' Saunders, a wild-eyed man who had never been seen to smile. Although his bark usually turned out to be worse than his bite, Saunders would hold back classes until every piece of equipment had been accounted for. His most well-used phrase was, 'Nobody leaves; there's a scriber missing.' One day, someone slipped a scriber into the pocket of his white coat, so when he counted up at the end, he went potty. The joke was on us, of course, because we were the ones being delayed and, obviously, no one dared suggest, 'Look in your pocket, Mr Saunders.' About half an hour elapsed before he obviously had to be somewhere else and let us go. Because I was actually scared of the machinery, metalwork lessons held a particular dread for me as Saunders had absolutely no sympathy for anyone who couldn't do a perfect job. He seemed such an insensitive man that it surprised me to learn that he was a keen gardener who exhibited at local flower shows. Bill Saunders lived in Slater Avenue, off Ashbourne Road, and there was great joy one day when a rumour swept his charges that he'd been assaulted on his way to school over an argument about a dog. In direct contrast to the others, Albert Haynes Pipes, who taught woodwork and technical drawing, was a meek and mild man who often had to summon the aid of Hanlon or Saunders to quell a rebellious class. Incidentally, under the stage name of Angela Piper, Albert's actress daughter has spent the last thirty-eight years in the BBC radio series *The Archers*.

When it came to any of the handicraft subjects I was completely incompetent but, somehow, I reached the fifth form still having to take metalwork. When the first metalwork lesson (a dreaded double period) of the 1960–61 school year loomed, I decided that my time could be better spent. On that first morning, while everyone else trailed across to Albany Road after morning break, I walked purposefully into the school library and took down a copy of *Citizen's Derby* by W. Alfred Richardson. Although my father was always keen to walk around sites of local historical interest, it was the first time I'd read anything on the subject. I was absorbed in the book when I felt a tap on my shoulder. It was Bill Pickering, an English master who was in charge of the library. Bill had a breathless, excitable manner, as well as a limp, all possibly because he'd spent three and a half years as a prisoner of the Japanese after being captured while serving with the Sherwood Foresters at the fall of Singapore.

Old Bemrosians reunion, 1986. Back row, left to right: Derek Weaver, John Mackenzie, Graham Roome, Tony White, David Donnelly, Arthur Auger, Stuart Clay, Tony Fry. Front row: Malc Spare, Colin Barson, John Cheadle, me, John Stewart, Mick Ellis. (Author's Collection)

'What are you doing?' he asked. 'Why aren't you in your lesson? Where should you be?'

I mumbled something about having hurt my hand and therefore not being fit for metalwork. He seemed satisfied and wandered off to attend to a delivery of new books. When everyone else arrived back at lunchtime, I asked Barry Iremonger if I'd been missed.

'No,' he said, 'Saunders never asked where you were.'

That was good enough for me. The next week I followed the same routine. Bill Pickering eyed me up again, but this time, to my surprise, didn't bother me. Over the course of the next nine months, I must have read dozens of books in that library, which no doubt did me more good than trying to tap a thread. So it was with some amazement that, in June 1961, I discovered that I'd been entered for the metalwork O-Level. The woodwork O-Level was scheduled for the same morning. I went to the library as usual and when Stuart Clay returned from his woodwork exam, with a free afternoon ahead of us we headed off for Nottingham Road to watch Derbyshire play Leicestershire in the County Cricket Championship. When I arrived at school the next day, I was asked why I'd not turned up for the metalwork exam. I said I'd felt unwell and then Herbert Cook astounded me: 'Mr Saunders is disappointed. He says it will be a snip pass for you. It's been arranged for you sit the exam tomorrow.' I was on the verge of suggesting that this was obviously a case of mistaken identity, but thought better of it. Did it really matter? I was leaving school in a matter of days. In the end, no-one told me where to go for the exam, or at what time, so I assumed that it was a joke at my expense. A few days later I walked down the East Drive of Bemrose School for the very last time.

CHAPTER SEVEN

Journeys with My Father

My father was a man of few words. He was what, in the 1950s, could be described as a working-class Tory. He read the *Daily Mail*, chuntered on about 'Labourites', and harked back to the good old days before nationalisation, when everyone was happy enough simply to know where they stood. When, in the scorching summer of 1959, there was a national printing dispute which compelled him to come out on strike together with the rest of his colleagues at the *Derby Evening Telegraph*, he chuntered about that too. It would be hard to imagine a less

Visiting schoolboys gather around my father's linotype machine at the Derby Evening Telegraph *in 1937. (Author's Collection)*

likely union activist than my father, but he was also a realist; he wouldn't have had a job to return to, had he ignored the instructions of the National Graphical Association. Life was difficult for those on the picket line. Strike pay was negligible, which meant that the Rippon household had to tighten its collective belt. The first thing to go was tobacco, although one Sunday evening my father caused pandemonium when he lit his pipe in the house and my mother thought the chimney was on fire. Desperate for a smoke, he'd gone mooching into the back garden, filled his pipe with dried rose leaves, then returned to puff contentedly on the result, which, of course, was a mini-bonfire. My mother's response made for an interesting accompaniment to the hymns being sung with such reverence on the Light Programme's *Sunday Half Hour*. The Sunday joint also had to go for the duration of the strike; when the dispute was finally over and the first full pay packets were distributed, I was sent straight to the butcher's to buy a large piece of sirloin.

But if the strike deprived him of his tobacco, the one thing that the six-week dispute did give my father was plenty of time to indulge in walking round Derby to discover the town's history. We'd been doing this ever since I could remember and it had given me a real appetite for learning about my home town. Now he had ample opportunity to stride out across the town and further afield. His favourite walk, which we did scores of times, took us up Irongate and into Queen Street, past the sixteenth-century timber-framed Nottingham Castle inn, through St Alkmund's churchyard and then across Bridgegate. Since the area was demolished to make way for a section of the inner ring road – has there been a greater act of civic vandalism, even in Derby? – it's been almost impossible to

My father and me on one of our many walks. This photograph may have been taken in Skegness, where we went for the day from Friargate station. (Author's Collection)

St Alkmund's churchyard with its Georgian houses, pictured before the inner ring road destroyed the area. (Don Farnsworth)

stand on the edge of that concrete canyon and imagine the elegant churchyard of trees and Georgian houses that once graced this part of the town. We'd continue up North Parade before dropping down by the side of the Great Northern railway line that ran into Friargate station. Where the line crossed the River Derwent, over Handyside's bridge, there was also a footbridge that could be the one unpleasant part of the walk. If we were unlucky enough to be on the bridge when a steam train came roaring past on its way into Derby, the likelihood was that we'd get covered in smoke and bits of burning cinder. The path then hugged the works of E.W. Bliss, who made presses for companies such as Heinz, and soon we'd be on City Road and into Darley Fields. On summer Saturdays we'd stop to watch the cricket played between clubs with such names as Amarilla, Centurions, Derby and Midland Mills, and Grasshoppers.

I was fascinated by the area's Roman past and it took little imagination to conjure up the fort near Chester Green. On Parker's Piece, where Derby School played their football and cricket, twentieth-century excavations had revealed that a large Roman house with the equivalent of under-floor central heating had once stood there. Little Chester had once been a rural community on the outskirts of Derby and people who'd grown up there in the 1920s and '30s said that it really was like living out in the country. There was certainly a rural feel to Darley Abbey, where a toll booth still displayed the individual cost of taking cows, pigs and sheep back across the Derwent. The eighteenth-century cotton and paper mills at Darley Abbey were now used by other businesses but the weir, built to help maintain the height of the river which served the mills, was as dramatic then as ever. For 200 years, Derbeians have been leaning against the railings to watch the Derwent turn white as soap suds as it roars over the weir at Darley. In Darley Park, the eighteenth-century Darley Hall was home to the Central School for Boys. When the hall was demolished in 1962, my father chuntered for many a long day about council vandalism, just as he did two years later when they also knocked down Markeaton Hall; and just as he had for years before, after the council flattened the Old Mayor's Parlour in Tenant Street. A spectacular remnant of Derby's medieval past, it was pulled down in 1948 and I can't say that I remember it all that well, but I grew up knowing that its demolition had been a public scandal.

The walk up Ashbourne Road to Markeaton Park had long been another favourite, not least because we generally stopped at a shop on the corner of Windmill Hill Lane for what was the best ice-cream I'd ever tasted; apparently it was made at the back of the premises. Like Darley Park, Markeaton Park had been given to the people of Derby by the town's landed gentry; and, like Darley, the council allowed the park's fine home to fall into such disrepair that razing it to the ground became the best option. Over the years, successive Derby administrations have been harshly criticised but the councillors who sanctioned the destruction of these two jewels in the civic crown deserve to be singled out for special vilification. What would a city of Derby's size give to have two such splendid mansions these days? The other highlight at Markeaton Park was the ten-minute ride on the motor boat which left a little landing stage and pottered among the rowing boats on the lake. I always wished that it would call at the island in the middle of the lake; there had to be Red Indians camped there somewhere.

My father also kept an eye out for special events. One of our Sunday afternoon outings was to Jury Street fire station where the local brigade occasionally gave demonstrations, usually by pumping clouds of smoke into a canvas tower and then going up on a turntable ladder and 'rescuing' one of their colleagues. One Saturday we were walking up Cheapside when a fire engine came round the corner, a fireman ringing its bell by pulling on a rope. As the engine sped towards Macklin Street, a brass hose coupling fell into the road. My father picked it up and marched into the fire station, dumped the coupling on the counter with a curt, 'One of your mates has just dropped this.' And marched out again. A man of few words was the old man.

On a Saturday afternoon in October 1954 there was a pageant to mark the granting to Derby of a market charter. It was described as the 800th anniversary of 'the town's first charter'. In fact, no one knew exactly when Henry II had awarded this to Derby, so the council elected to stage its celebrations 800 years after the start of that monarch's reign, which seemed fair enough. The main event was a cavalcade through the town watched by thousands of Derbeians, me included. The parade route stretched from Bass's Rec to Markeaton Park, and was led by bands from the Sherwood Foresters and the Borough Police. Local businesses put on dozens of colourful floats and there was a parade of appliances representing 200 years of fire-fighting in Derby; firemen joined in by wearing historical uniforms, as did local policemen. The whole thing was finished off with a horse-drawn tram, and even a horse-drawn street-sweeping machine. The mayor, Alderman Alec Ling, rode in an open horse-drawn carriage, doffing his hat to one and all. At Markeaton Park, there was a sheep roasting. It sounds simple fun, but don't forget: the last of wartime rationing had been lifted a mere three months earlier.

On wet days we'd sometimes go no further than the Museum and Art Gallery in the Wardwick, spending a couple of hours looking at familiar exhibits. The model train ran only on Saturday mornings, but my absolute favourite was a model of how Derby had looked in the eighteenth century. There were a few familiar landmarks – All Saints', St Michael's, St Peter's, and St Werburgh's churches, mostly – but what an intriguing exhibit it was. I tried to find the area in which we lived. I could make out the well-worn path that would eventually become Abbey Street, but everything else was just fields.

Longer walks took us to Derby Airport at Burnaston, on the road to Burton, a good four miles from our house. The giant Toyota factory now covers the site; fifty years ago it was home to the Dakotas of Derby Airways who took the more affluent Derbeians to exotic places like Jersey. I never dared to dream of enjoying such a luxury. The airport had been opened in 1939 – one of Derby Town Council's better moments – but became an RAF station when war was declared. Back in peacetime, the airport would occasionally advertise a pleasure flight but, again, I never harboured any realistic hopes that we would be going up for a spin. One of the last people I remember using the old airport, before it was replaced by the former bomber station at Castle Donington, was my old school pal Terry King, who used to fly in from Belfast (he was stationed at RAF Ballykelly in Northern Ireland) and then simply walk home to his parents' house in Bretton Avenue, Littleover.

We usually went to Burnaston on a Sunday afternoon, which was just as well because Sundays in 1950s Derby were about as boring as it is possible to imagine. There were no shops open, save little corner stores and off-licences, and even they had to observe strict opening hours. The 1950 Shops Act also prohibited the sale of some items but not other, often similar, goods. For instance, you could buy tinned peas but not fresh ones. And you could buy a magazine but not a book, which meant that it was illegal to sell a copy of the Holy Bible on a Sunday although you could buy a saucy mag. How daft was that? Cinemas opened, but only briefly, and no God-fearing person would be seen going to the pictures on a Sunday. So after the Light Programme's lunchtime diet of *Two-Way Family Favourites*, *The Billy Cotton Band Show* and *Educating Archie*, it was either a game of ludo or a good stiff walk. The weather had to be particularly bad for my father not to suggest the latter option. The wireless, though, played an enormous part in my growing up. It always seemed to be on in our house. *Take It from Here, Hancock's Half Hour, Life with the Lyons, The Navy Lark, The Al Reed Show, Meet the Huggetts, Much*

Binding in the March, Journey into Space, Dick Barton, Variety Bandbox, Riders of the Range, Workers' Playtime, Have a Go, Ray's a Laugh – I lapped up the lot. There were also some odd programmes on the radio, not least the occasional circus. How bizarre it seems now, to have sat listening intently to someone describing a trapeze artist, a juggler or a lion tamer that you couldn't see.

This was probably why we never missed a live circus or a fair on Bass's Rec. The circuses were run by Bertram Mills or the Chipperfield Brothers and involved braving a close encounter with something called 'the Derby Hum'. In all its glory, the Hum permeated every facet of the town's life. It was the smell of burning bones emanating from the slaughterhouse at the Cattle Market next door to Bass's Rec. Queuing up to get into a circus brought you right up close and personal. There was a joke that when, in 1745, Bonnie Prince Charlie got as far as Derby before deciding to give up his march on London and the throne, it was the Derby Hum that really put him off. Two hundred years later, the Hum wasn't the only unpleasant smell to hang over the town: the stench of chemicals from the British Celanese works at Spondon was also powerful enough to send people hurrying indoors; for some reason, it was particularly pungent on a cold winter's morning. But braving the Hum was worth it if it meant a night at the circus. The evening began with a walk over the bridge that spanned Derby Canal, where, for years, lay the rotting remains of a barge. Then we snaked onwards into the Big Top. I loved the circus: the ringmaster with his red coat, top hat and whip; the performing animals (these were less enlightened times); trapeze artists and jugglers; and the clowns, most of all the clowns. There was always a car that exploded, and all sorts of slapstick humour. The fairs also had a wonderful atmosphere, although one attraction that I wasn't old enough to enter was the boxing booth where challengers from the crowd could win 10s if they managed three rounds with the grizzled old ex-pro who'd probably been thrown out of legal boxing for throwing a fight or shoving a horseshoe in his glove. I doubt if anyone ever came away with a ten-bob note.

In winter we exchanged the circus and the fair for the warmth of the cinema or the Hippodrome Theatre. Derby boasted perhaps twenty cinemas, ranging from town-centre venues like the Gaumont on London Road, the Odeon in St Peter's Street, the Regal in East Street (where a theatre organist and his organ would suddenly rise out of the floor) and the Picture House in Babington Lane, to suburban cinemas like the Cavendish in Normanton, the Rex at Alvaston and the Essoldo at Chaddesden. Our nearest cinema was the Black Prince in Colyear Street. Even the notorious West End had its own cinema, the Popular in Mill Street. I loved western films and the 1950s there was no shortage of these starring people like John Wayne, James Stewart, Jeff Chandler and Audie Murphy. I was thrilled when cinemas experimented with 3D films. We had to wear special spectacles – one red lens, one green – and then dived all over the place as knives and flaming arrows appeared to come shooting out of the screen. My mother had more sophisticated tastes and loved opera, so when the film *The Great Caruso* starring Mario Lanza came to the Odeon in 1951, she came along too. It would be impossible for today's youngsters to imagine the thrill of going to the cinema in the 1950s. Few homes had a television, and, on top of that, few homes, if any, boasted the kind of luxury that greeted you at the cinema: central heating, bright lights, chandeliers, luxurious carpets – it was like stepping into another world. The only downside, so far as I was concerned, was the continuous performance where the main film and the 'B' movie (usually a black and white British cop drama), together with the newsreel, just kept rolling from 2 p.m. until the stampede to beat the National Anthem at about 10 p.m. My father was a man who wouldn't be hurried, so instead of dashing to make the start of the main feature, we'd always arrive in the middle of the film. The whole programme would continue until the point I always dreaded, when my father would nudge me and say, 'I think this is where we came in.' Up we'd get and stumble out in the dark. I always saw the second half of films before I saw the first; I think I was about thirteen before I saw a big film from beginning to end.

The Hippodrome Theatre was in Green Lane, just a five-minute walk from home. We always went to the pantomime, but also to all the variety shows to see many of the great comedy legends: Jimmy James; Jimmy Wheeler; Albert Modley; Stan Stennett; Nat Jackley; Arthur English. My favourites, though, were Wilson, Keppel and Betty who today would surely be banned as politically incorrect. Jack Wilson, Joe Keppel and Betty Knox had a stage act called the 'sand dance', a ludicrous parody of

The Hippodrome Theatre in Green Lane, where we queued up to see the great comedians and singers of the 1950s. (Author's Collection)

The Grand Theatre in Babington Lane closed down in 1949, but not before I had managed to be sick during a performance there. (Author's Collection)

'Egyptian' postures, combined with stereotyped references to Arabic costume (they wore fezzes and long robes). Apparently the act had been going since 1910 (they wouldn't retire until 1963) and there were, in fact, three 'Bettys', with Knox's daughter, and then granddaughter, taking over the role. I loved to hear the orchestra tuning up. As soon as the lights went on in the orchestra pit, and those first discordant notes of the violins rent the air, I settled down in my seat in anticipation of what was about to unfold. In the late 1950s, the Hippodrome, like almost all provincial theatres, found the competition presented by television too much. After limping on for a while with nude revues with such titles as *Strip, Strip Ahoy – The Biggest Navel Show in the Midlands* (alas, I never got to see any of those) the Hippodrome became a bingo hall. Thankfully, the bingo company did very little to the theatre's splendid interior and so there are still plenty of Derbeians who cherish the probably forlorn hope that the grand old place may one day be turned over again to live theatre. If it happens, I'll be first in the queue. Incidentally, I'd also been taken to the Grand Theatre in Babington Lane before it closed in 1949; I don't remember anything about it but grew up with the tale of how I was sick during the performance. Maybe I should have become a theatre critic.

One day my father decided to go much further afield to broaden my appreciation of life. We were stopping in Spalding when he decided to take me and one of my cousins, Gwen, to London for the day. We did all the usual sights – Houses of Parliament, Buckingham Palace and so on – and had egg and chips at a Lyons Corner House in Leicester Square, but

Outside Buckingham Palace in 1950. The same day we went to see the bomb-damaged East End. (Author's Collection)

then we caught a bus to the East End to see the damage wrought by Hitler's Blitz. It was five years after the end of the Second World War but huge areas still bore witness to the devastation. Many bomb sites had been cleared, but there were still plenty of ruined houses, just shells really. My most enduring memory, however, is of seeing a small band of street musicians, all disabled ex-servicemen who had fought the war, playing for pennies. The whole experience made a long-lasting impression on me.

Mostly, however, our weekends were spent wandering around Derby, sometimes exploring new areas, but mostly treading familiar and favoured paths. Homeward bound, we'd stop off at the Open Market in the Morledge where, on dark Saturday teatimes in midwinter, traders would be selling off the last of their vegetables at knockdown prices. On nearby Cockpit Hill, Mad Harry would be smashing up tea sets and crying, "I'm not asking for two pounds, I'm not asking for thirty bob, I'm not even asking for a pound – ten and six for this lovely service.' Then a 'plant' in the crowd would step forward and 'buy' one. If one or two genuine punters didn't then join in, Mad Harry would simply throw the whole lot to the ground. It was great entertainment. Then off we'd stroll, up East Street, on into St Peter's Churchyard, up Green Lane, down Wilson Street, up Gerard Street, and home for tea.

Those long walks also gave me an opportunity to get to know my father better because, for the first few years of my life, his job at the *Long Eaton Advertiser* meant that I saw very little of him. Alec Rippon was born in 1905, in the Cambridgeshire town of March where my grandfather, Joe Rippon, ran a barber's shop that also doubled as a tobacconist's and fishing tackle shop. The family moved to Reading, then, on the eve of the First World War, to Cromer on the Norfolk coast, and finally back to Spalding from where Joe's family hailed. As a boy my father made his pocket money by intercepting well-to-do travellers at Spalding railway station and carrying their bags to one of the town's commercial hotels.

Other revenue was generated by working as my grandfather's lather boy at his shop in Francis Street. The God-fearing men of the town would leave the pub on a Saturday night and be shaved and waxed ready for church the next morning. My grandfather would be wielding his razor, my father his lather brush until midnight.

I came to love Spalding, spending most Augusts there. The journey began with a rare taxi ride when the Fordhyre company in Mount Street ran us to Derby Midland station (which still showed signs of wartime bomb damage) for 2s; when the fare went up to 2s 6d, my father briefly considered walking instead. At Nottingham Midland we changed to a train bound for Great Yarmouth. Every time we went into a tunnel someone had to jump out of their seat to pull up the carriage window, otherwise the compartment would have been filled with smoke. It probably didn't matter. The carriages were usually so dirty that when anyone sat down, clouds of dust billowed up from the upholstery. On one occasion a previous traveller had whiled away their journey with a pencil, decorating the carriage ceiling and walls with obscene graffiti, explicit drawings and all. The train was packed and there was no opportunity to move, so everyone sat there and tried not to look at the handiwork. At least the view out of the window was pleasant enough: fields of ripening corn with, every so often, two men in white overalls carrying a ladder through a field of cows (the men were made of wood and advertised a brand of paint). At Bourne our steam loco had a ride on a turntable before chugging on to the pretty fenland station at Twenty hamlet with its immaculate garden and neat row of bright red fire buckets filled with sand.

By the time we arrived at Spalding Town station, its gas lamps were beginning to glow. And at 17 Spring Gardens, sitting in the same chair year after year, there was the regal figure of Gran Rippon wearing a black dress and grey cardigan, the likes of which she'd donned every day since Joe had died twenty years earlier. The Rippons were living in the fenland Deepings, near Spalding, way back in the 1700s. In 1861 my great-grandfather, William Rippon, a twenty-year-old blacksmith, was staying with his widowed mother in Deeping St James. Work took him to Spilsby where his next-door neighbour was the town crier. Eventually, he finished up living in Churchgate, Spalding, with his wife and four sons. Spalding in the 1950s was very different from Derby. If the railway station was still lit by gas lamps, so was Gran's house. On hot summer evenings, we'd hang on for as long as possible before lighting the gas mantles because they generated a fair amount of extra heat. Only when dusk threatened did Uncle Jim, my father's brother, put a lighted taper to the gas jet. Jim's wife, Ivy, a jolly Essex girl he'd met in the Army, would put the kettle on, bring out the cheese and pickles, and we'd have supper. Quite how we managed to eat so much, I don't know. Large cooked breakfasts were followed by roast joint lunches with rib-sticking puddings. Teas consisted of huge meat salads, bread and butter and home-made cakes. And then these hearty suppers just before we turned in. It was a wonder that anyone slept.

Each day we'd set off on an adventure: a four-mile round walk to Pinchbeck to see the village stocks; or to Pode Hole because the name amused us; sometimes we'd tackle the eight-mile round trip to Cowbit.

We caught the bus to Skegness, to Hunstanton and to Uncle Albert's farm at Bicker Fen, near Boston. When I was older, my father returned home after his fortnight's holiday – my mother rarely came to Spalding as she had her own mother to care for – and I'd be left with Gran Rippon until it was time for me to go back to junior school in Derby in September. After breakfast, with an ocean of a day ahead of me, I'd set off to explore anew. I'd walk and walk, out of the town, down country lanes and alongside dykes. The huge skies of South Lincolnshire fascinated me. I'd sit by a hedgerow to eat the home-made cake that Gran had packed for me, and occasionally some old boy trudging in the opposite direction would stop and ask me where I was going. If they weren't in a hurry – and no-one ever appeared to be in a hurry – they'd volunteer to tell me what it had been like around here in years gone by. Probably much the same, I used to think. Sometimes they'd tell me about the war. Not the one just ended, but the one before that.

Derby Evening Telegraph *staff pictured outside the old Northcliffe House in June 1958 on their way to Nottingham races. My father is sixth from the left. Standing behind him in the bus doorway is sportswriter Wilf Shaw. Fourth from left is John Bowers, an advertising rep who played part-time professional football for Derby County. Third from left is Malcolm Edmondson, a compositor. Bill Heseltine of the circulation department is second from right. (Author's Collection)*

My father was nine when the First World War broke out, so he had vivid memories of the conflict as it unfolded. He'd pored over maps showing troop movements, fought battles with his lead soldiers, collected money to send comforts to soldiers on the Western Front (the townsfolk of Spalding rewarded his patriotism with a certificate) and on one occasion stumbled across a 'spy' on the cliff top at Cromer. It was a winter's day in 1915 and he was out walking with my grandfather when they spotted a man using a pair of binoculars, apparently signalling out to sea. My grandfather reckoned that the man was a German spy working with a U-boat. They set off for Cromer police station and reported the matter. Of course, they were never made aware of the outcome. The man with the binoculars was probably just looking for the lesser black-backed gull. You couldn't be too careful in wartime, though, said my father.

In fact, in the 1950s, England was a country in which the First World War, never mind the Second, still stirred plenty of memories. Those who had fought in what was normally referred to as the Great War were working men, still some way short of their pension; because of that, the 1914–18 conflict still felt near enough to reach out and touch. Indeed, there were veterans of the Boer War still about. The majority of those who had seen action between 1939 and 1945 were relatively young men in their late twenties and early thirties. In fact, life seemed dominated by those wars which had taken up a significant part of the twentieth century. And when he wasn't remembering one war or another, or exploring Derby's history, or queuing up for the circus on Bass's Rec, or the Hippodrome, there was one overriding passion that took up a fair portion of my father's life . . .

CHAPTER EIGHT

It Should Be a Good Match . . .

It was 20 December 1953 – my ninth birthday – when my father came home at lunchtime from the *Long Eaton Advertiser* and, as the fish and chips were being plated up, announced that we were going to the match. It was to be my first-team debut at the Baseball Ground. He'd already taken me to a few reserve-team matches, but this was the big-time. Derby County were playing Bolton Wanderers in the First Division. 'Nat Lofthouse is playing for Bolton; it should be a good game', the old man told me as we finished our treacle tart and custard.

The walk to the Baseball Ground was always the same: along Gerard Street, across Burton Road and up Mount Street, then Normanton Road, Harriet Street, through the Arboretum, left into Rosehill Street, down Malcolm Street (where householders stored bicycles for 3*d* for the afternoon) and into Colombo Street which led straight to the turnstiles for the Osmaston End of the Popular Side. Just to confuse me, on the way was Molineux Street: I wondered if that was where Wolves played. What was different on this day was the crowd. Reserve matches attracted perhaps 2,000 spectators; today, as it turned out, there would be almost 13,000. That might still seem a small crowd by today's standards, but Derby County were struggling (and it was the last shopping Saturday before Christmas). It had been only seven years since the Rams had won the FA Cup at Wembley in the first postwar Final, but that fine team had gradually broken up and, despite twice breaking the British transfer record in the late 1940s, by coronation year the team had dropped down the league table. The previous season the Rams had just about managed to stave off relegation but, by this December day, they had won only four matches of their new campaign. I'd had my ears filled with tales of Raich Carter and Peter Doherty, and before them the likes of Sammy Crooks, Jack Barker and Dally Duncan. It was the memories of these names that now sustained supporters in such bleak times.

I'd like to say that I recall all the details of that match against Bolton but, of course, I was far too young to appreciate the game or the style of the players. I remember that Reg Harrison and the burly Jack Stamps, both of whom had gained Cup winners' medals with Derby at Wembley (Stamps had scored two Cup Final goals) were playing because my father pointed them out. And Bert Mozley, who had played for England in the

Boys' enclosure at the Baseball Ground in the early 1950s. (Raymond's News Agency)

Rams' better days, was at right-back. Another former England player, Jack Lee, was at centre-forward and scored a goal as Derby won 4–3. It was probably a real thriller; alas, I can't remember. Just as, although I can say that I saw Nat Lofthouse play, to be honest, I have no recollection of him. My only clear memory of that chilly afternoon is the smell: a heady aroma of bay rum hair dressing, Brylcreem and cigarette smoke. Years later, through working with BBC Radio Derby, I would become good friends with Messrs Harrison, Stamps and Mozley. Jack and Norah Stamps would invite us to their golden wedding party, while Bert and Jean Mozley would one day show us round the beautiful Canadian city of Victoria. I would also manage to play against Jack and Reg in a couple of charity matches. All that, though, was a long way in the future and I couldn't have imagined any of it as we shuffled out of the ground, stamping the life back into our frozen feet, everyone around us buzzing at an unexpected

Derby victory. Six days later we were back for a Boxing Day game against Portsmouth. Again, Derby won, this time by 3–0, and I began to wonder why everyone was worrying. It was, however, just a blip; by the end of the season the Rams were rock bottom of the table and relegated to play in the Second Division for the first time in almost thirty years.

By now we were going regularly, but things at the Baseball Ground were going from bad to worse, and in 1955 the team finished bottom again and were sent spinning into the Third Division's Northern Section. In fact, this turned out to be my favourite era in Derby County's history. By the time Brian Clough was weaving his magic in the late 1960s and early 1970s, I was compelled to work on most Saturdays, so I saw relatively few games in that period. But the years 1955 to 1957 were just wonderful. A new manager, Harry Storer, who had played for the club in the 1920s, had taken over and built a team that combined the skill of players like veterans Tommy Powell and Reg Ryan (an Irish international who, the previous year, had won an FA Cup winner's medal with West Brom) with the muck-and-nettles approach of defenders like Martin McDonnell, a former paratrooper whose party piece was a sliding tackle followed by a couple of forward rolls for effect. McDonnell was so tough that he once played for a month with a broken bone in his foot and never bothered to tell anyone. My favourite player, though, was Tommy Powell. I doubt if there has ever been a player with better ball control than Tommy, who could kill even the highest, fiercest pass from a less skilful teammate and then, with the ball completely under his control, set off, leaving some hapless full-back from Workington or Gateshead in his wake. Tommy had been moved out to the right wing, so he took the corners at the Osmaston End of the Popular Side where we stood. The bottom of the terrace was actually below the level of the pitch (which itself was below street level) so I'd scramble down, look up at my hero's knees as he went to swing the ball over. Then, at the top of my voice, I'd shout, 'Come on, Tommy', hoping that, in some way, it might just give him that tiny bit extra and it would make all the difference.

By now the atmosphere at the Baseball Ground was much better. Attendances had picked up to over 20,000 for most home games, and when Derby's greatest rivals for promotion, Grimsby Town, came in March 1956, there were over 33,000 of us packed inside. For this match my father had decided to spend 3s 6d each on two tickets for the top deck of the Osmaston Stand. Seat tickets were at a premium but my father worked part-time as a tote operator at Derby's greyhound stadium where the tote manager was Alec Miller who was also Derby County's assistant secretary. There was an extra buzz in the streets around the Baseball Ground that Saturday lunchtime. The *Derby Evening Telegraph*'s matchday edition, sold by a newspaper seller with an uncanny resemblance to Arthur Askey (and whose rallying cry was 'Derby's team – and what a bloody team!'), was disappearing like hot cakes, the residents of Malcolm Street and Colombo Street were wondering where they were going to store all the extra bikes, and corner shops were doing a roaring trade in cigarettes and cough sweets. It was a vital match because only one team could be promoted, and everyone was nervous. My greatest impression of the match was that the Grimsby players all looked like giants. Their player-manager, Allenby Chilton, a former star with Manchester United, had signed some big defenders and one of them, a Channel Islander called Ray de Gruchy, tackled Derby's leading scorer, Jack Parry, so hard that Parry had to be helped from the pitch and didn't play again that season. As substitutes weren't allowed in those days, the Rams had to carry on with only ten men, and Grimsby won 3–1. They were a good side, though, and thoroughly deserved to win promotion.

The Grimsby game wasn't the first time that we'd sat in the stands at the Baseball Ground. The previous November, Derby had been drawn at home to a non-League club, Boston United, in the FA Cup. It was a headline writer's dream because Boston included six former Derby County players including Reg Harrison, the 1946 Cup winner. No-one, of course, gave Boston a chance because they were what were known as footballing 'minnows' who played in the Midland League. Ironically, given that I had become such an avid Derby County supporter, I also had a huge soft spot for Boston United because my Uncle Albert owned a farm not far from the town. So when the minnows won by the astonishing scoreline of 6–1 that was the moment when I realised the true meaning of mixed emotions. The following season, though, it was laughter all the way as Derby again scored over 100 goals and this time won promotion.

From the beginning of that 1956/7 season until December 1964, when I had to start working on Saturday afternoons, I didn't miss a home

This dog-eared cutting from the Derby Evening Telegraph *shows Colin Shaw (lower right, no tie), next to him Fred Brough (in cap) and me (mac, scarf and tie) at the Baseball Ground in December 1959. The man with the white square around his head won 10s 6d. Colin suggested taking his own wooden frame to the next match. (Derby Evening Telegraph)*

match at the Baseball Ground. In the summer of 1956 my father had moved to the *Derby Evening Telegraph* which meant that he could rarely get to football because the newspaper operated a rolling day-off system – Monday one week, Tuesday the next, and so on – and so Colin Shaw became my regular Saturday afternoon companion. We had a routine – call it a ritual – in which I would call round at his house, his mother, Dolly, would yell upstairs, 'Anton's here', and he would shout back, 'I'm just looking for a white shirt in case they're short.' It always made me laugh, anyway. We still took the same route and went to both first-team and reserve matches. Derby's reserves played in the strong Central League against the second teams of the leading northern clubs such as Manchester United, Liverpool and Newcastle United. This meant that we would often be treated to star players who were regaining full fitness after injury; I remember seeing Duncan Edwards and Tommy Taylor, both of whom were to perish in the 1958 Munich air disaster, turning out for Manchester United's reserves.

Everyone says that they know where they were when they heard that President Kennedy had been assassinated in November 1963. On a cold February teatime in 1958, Colin Shaw and I were taking refuge in the doorway of Scrimshaw's fish and chip shop, next to Tommy Harris's emporium in Boyer Street, when Mr Scrimshaw himself came from behind the counter and headed towards us. We thought he was going to tell us to stop littering the entrance to his business premises, but instead he asked, 'Have you heard the news, lads?' Manchester United's aircraft carrying them back from a European Cup match in Belgrade had crashed while trying to take off from a snow-bound runway in Munich, killing twenty-three people including eight United stars. One of them was the young England giant, Duncan Edwards, who died almost a fortnight after the crash. 'All flights cancelled. Flying home tomorrow. Duncan', read the telegram which arrived at his landlady's house in Manchester at about the same time as we were huddled in Scrimshaw's doorway. If only. My mind went back to the autumn evening I'd seen him lording it over the Baseball Ground as he got back to match fitness.

There was hardly any televised football, so to see international players in the flesh was a rare treat. In fact, with no blanket coverage of the game – no local radio, mobile phone score flashes and all the things we have become used to in the twenty-first century – it was often difficult to keep up to date with the Rams' scorelines when they were playing away. Going to a reserve match helped. There was a scoreboard at either end of the Baseball Ground, a sort of big wooden frame with letters A to L. In the match programme each of these letters was assigned to a Football League match from that afternoon's schedule, and at half-time a man would emerge to post up the latest scores. In the case of Derby's matches, however, he would come out whenever a goal had been scored, so there was always an excited chatter in the crowd when he opened the door of his hut. Occasionally, he would wind up the small crowd by pretending to post a goal in the opposing team's slot, and then quickly switch it to Derby's. I don't think he would ever have dared to do it the other way round.

With my heroes. A 1993 reunion of the Rams' 1957 Northern Section championship side saw me muscle in on the photograph. From left to right are Terry Webster, Dennis Woodhead, Reg Ryan, me, Tommy Powell and Ray Young. (Neil Simpson)

The latter half of the 1950s and the first half of the 1960s saw Derby County bumping along happily enough in the Second Division. Harry Storer retired, to be replaced by another former Rams playing favourite, Tim Ward, who had played for England in the late 1940s. Tim was a nice man, and a good manager too, but he suffered at the hands of a parsimonious Derby County board. It was Tim who was responsible for signing Kevin Hector, who went on to become one of the club's greatest players; yet when Hector was taken ill with jaundice, one Rams director asked Tim, 'Do we still have to pay his wages if he's ill and can't play?' That was a measure of how small-minded they all were. Eventually, in May 1967, Tim was sacked and Brian Clough took over. The resultant years have been well catalogued and bear no repetition here. Tim, in the meantime, took over as manager of Carlisle United before moving into industry. We became friends when I was working on a radio series on Derby County's history and I helped him to form the ex-Rams players' association. Tim's son, Andrew, also became a close friend and we went on to collaborate on several books. Such is the nature of sport: it provides such long-lasting bonds.

About the same time that my father introduced me to football, he also showed me what cricket was all about. In June 1953, we went to Trent Bridge to see England play Australia in the First Test. This was the

Australian side of Ray Lindwall and Keith Miller, Lindsey Hassett and Richie Benaud, while Len Hutton, Denis Compton and Godfrey Evans were in the England team. Again, I can remember nothing about the game other than the overall impression of this huge arena packed to the rafters. Of course, there was no Barmy Army with their inane chants. Just a reverent hush as the bowler came in to bowl, and then thunderous applause if the ball was struck well, or a wicket was taken. It all added up to much greater drama than can be found in today's game. The sight of Trent Bridge staging a Test Match was also a huge change from the normal scene at the County Ground, Derby, where the ramshackle former racecourse buildings were often home to no more than a few dozen spectators. Like Derby County, Derbyshire CCC provided me with my favourite players, most prominently the fast bowlers Cliff Gladwin and Les Jackson, and George Dawkes, Derbyshire's swashbuckling wicketkeeper. The captain, Guy Willatt, was an attractive left-handed batsman, if I remember correctly, but it was his replacement as skipper who really fascinated me. Donald Carr, a former Repton School pupil who had appeared in a Victory Test back in 1946 when he was still a schoolboy, was an elegant right-handed batsman but a cricketer who bowled left-handed, sending down these mysterious little 'Chinamen' as they were called. Sometimes he would get hit to all parts of the County Ground but occasionally he would bamboozle the best batsmen in the country. I liked Carr.

Watching – and, no doubt, playing – at the County Ground was not for the faint-hearted, certainly not on days when the weather was unkind. The wind would come whipping off the old racecourse, straight from the Urals it seemed, to cut through you like a knife (many years later the club partially solved the problem by erecting an earthen bank; hardly cutting-edge architecture, but effective enough). The facilities were awful: toilets that could best be described as French Colonial; pigeon droppings covering the seats in the former racecourse grandstand; and catering which made the worst that British Railways could offer look like a Savoy Grill buffet.

When I first visited the County Ground, the pitch was set well away from its present location and a Victorian pavilion provided changing and seating facilities. That was demolished in 1955, when the club decided to move the pitch nearer to the old grandstand. Our route there took us through the town centre, over the River Derwent at Exeter Bridge, then on up Nottingham Road, past the railway station and into Stores Road. Even after passing through the turnstile, there was still a few hundred yards' walk across the grass to reach the rickety tiered seating that must have been there since W.G. Grace was the main attraction. The County Ground was a dump in the real sense of the word, a place of gentle decay. It remained like that for decades. Today, it looks more like a decent cricket venue. It is just a pity that the game of cricket itself has lost its soul.

When we weren't walking to the Baseball Ground or the County Ground, we had plenty of other sporting venues to while away our Saturday afternoons. Rowditch Athletic was our local football team who played their Derby and District Senior League home matches on Rykneld Recreation Ground, sometimes attracting a four-figure attendance. And the West End

Just before Derbyshire's game against the South Africans at the ramshackle County Ground in May 1955, new spectator accommodation in the old racecourse grandstand was opened. (Author's Collection)

Boys' Club, who played on Markeaton Rec, were also worth a visit. Occasionally, we'd jump on a bus and travel to watch Belper Town, Matlock Town or Ilkeston Town in the Central Alliance, or go down to the old police athletic ground at the bottom of Sinfin Lane where Derby County's third team played in the same competition. In summer, if Derbyshire were playing away, there was always the local cricket on Darley Fields, and Derby Rowing Club's annual regatta on the Derwent was a must.

Every other Monday in winter, there was professional boxing at the King's Hall in Queen Street, where the council laid a floor over the swimming baths. Most of the shows were promoted by a Derby greengrocer, Frank Woodhouse, and many of the boxers were managed by a chap from Leicester called George Biddles, who later had a British heavyweight champion, Jack Bodell from Swadlincote, in his stable. In the 1950s, though, Biddles's most famous boxer was the Nigerian, Hogan 'Kid' Bassey, who won the world featherweight title in 1957. I saw Bassey fight on a bill at Derby and he was obviously a big draw because the King's Hall normally saw only little-known professionals. Nowadays, the number of active professional boxers in Britain is around 650, the majority of those semi-professional; there are only a few dozen who earn a full-time living in the sport. Back in the 1950s, there were probably 3,000 or more professional boxers, so many of those who fought in Derby were unknown. A former pro boxer lived near us in Gerard Street. Alec Drain had fought as a welterweight between 1937 and 1940; unsurprisingly, he used the name Alec Jackson for his professional bouts. He had long retired by the time I knew him, but the one thing I always noticed were his cauliflower ears. It was that kind of thing that I found so appealing about those nights at the boxing. It was brutal and it was slightly seedy. There are still amateur shows in Derby, but we'll never again see those regular fight nights in smoke-filled halls where men scrapped for a few extra pounds in order to make life a little better for their families. That's undoubtedly a good thing, but it did have a compelling edge to it. The same could never be said of all-in wrestling, which was also staged at the King's Hall. I went with Barry Iremonger to see if anyone could unmask the mysterious Count Bartelli. They couldn't, and it all looked fixed to me. Later I discovered that the legendary Count was, in fact, a bloke called Geoff Condliffe from Crewe, which reinforced my general amusement at this so-called sport. When I read that he was eventually 'unmasked' by someone called Kendo Nagasaki (Pete Thornley from Stoke to his friends), I was finally convinced that no one was supposed to take it seriously.

If it was the much more wholesome sport of athletics you wanted in the 1950s, then Derby and County Athletic Club, which had several international-class runners, staged some excellent meetings at the Municipal Sports Ground on Osmaston Park Road. The Municipal had always been a favourite with Derby's sporting fraternity. It was built by unemployed men who returned to Derby from the First World War to find that, instead of the promised land 'fit for heroes', there were no jobs waiting for them. The ground, erected on farm land, was opened in August 1923, and was soon the centre of controversy when several international cyclists declared the concrete track around the arena banking unfit for top-class racing because high speeds couldn't be reached because of the positioning of the bends. Derby County might have moved there. Later in 1923 there was talk of the Rams paying the council an annual rent of £500, together with a percentage of any increase over the average Baseball Ground gate money. A year later, however, the club bought the Baseball Ground outright.

The late 1920s and early 1930s saw a golden age of Derby sport, and the Municipal shared in the revival. Athletics, open-air boxing, soccer and rugby were all staged there. After closing down on the outbreak of the Second World War, Derby County resumed there in 1941 before moving back to the Baseball Ground later that year. Then, just after the war, with English football looking for a so-called 'Wembley of the North', Maxwell Ayrton, the architect of Wembley's original Empire Stadium, drew up plans to transform the Municipal into just such a venue. His scheme provided capacity for 78,600 spectators, and under the main grandstand there would have been housed a swimming pool, an indoor sports centre, gymnasium, dance hall and catering facilities. A vital part of the plan was for Derby County to leave the Baseball Ground, where they had played since 1895, and transfer to the Municipal Sports Ground. Eventually, the Rams decided to stay put, and the scheme foundered, although nearly thirty years later an indoor sports centre and a swimming pool were finally constructed on the site (and I went to work there). In the 1950s, we used to go there for the borough's school sports. In 2006, however, it was announced that the Municipal Sports Ground was to be demolished and houses built on the site instead. Even when it comes to sport, Derby's council has always seemed keen to demolish things.

CHAPTER NINE

Evenings around a Piano

In my last summer at school, I met the girl I was to marry. Pat Buckler was a friend of John Cheadle's sister, Linda, so that's how the introduction was made. I saw her around when I visited the Cheadles, or when she was playing tennis on the Co-op sports ground next to St Chad's cricket ground on Littleover Lane, where I turned out for Derby Red Rose. Then one Monday evening in late autumn that year, I decided to walk to the Cheadles rather than catch the no. 30, Browning Circle, bus, and halfway down Normanton Road, I bumped into Pat, who was waiting for the same bus to take her to Girl Guides at St Giles's Church Hall on Village Street. She decided to walk with me instead, and that was that. We started going out together that Christmas. I could never resist a uniform.

Just before being posted to Salonika during the First World War, Bill Poynton of the Derbyshire Yeomanry was photographed with his wife Annie and daughter Beatrice, the little girl who, fifty years later, became my mother-in-law. (Author's Collection)

Pat with her mum and dad on a family holiday at Scarborough in the 1950s. (Author's Collection)

Below: The ladies of Peartree and Normanton British Legion in the early 1960s. Beatrice Buckler is second from left on the front row. Pat is there too, standing directly in front of the middle one of the three ladies on the back row. (Author's Collection)

Pat's family were the nicest people you could ever wish to meet. They lived in Depot Street, off Normanton Road, and were an old Derby family. Her father, Bernard, was born in the Depot Street house just before the First World War; her mother, Beatrice Poynton, came from Cameron Road, near the Cavendish. Bernard worked at Rolls-Royce, along with his brother-in-law, Trevor Poynton, a Second World War veteran of the terrible Burma campaign, although Trevor never spoke of it despite suffering recurrent bouts of malaria. Pat's younger sister, Barbara, went to Homelands School. They were a musical family: Trevor played the cornet in the Rolls-Royce band, while Pat's mother sang in Royce's choir and was also a good pianist. One of the highlights of Christmas (apart from Beatrice's roast beef lunch) was the Boxing Day get-together

Boxing Day at Depot Street in 1970. Left to right are Kath and Trevor Poynton, Beatrice Buckler and a camera-conscious Nicola Rippon. (Author's Collection)

around the piano in the front room at Depot Street, where Pat's mum would play the music while everyone else, including her Auntie Doll and her cousin Joyce, joined in with the words. Looking back now, it seems a world away from the modern age: simple pleasures practised by God-fearing people. I was made to feel one of that wonderful family from the moment I first stepped through the door and in June 1968 Pat and I were married at St Giles's; the following year our daughter, Nicola, was born. She, too, was able to join in those Christmases and other family occasions at Depot Street before Pat's mum died suddenly in 1974. Nicola is a lucky girl to have those warm memories of an age that has now largely disappeared; there may, of course, still be dozens of Derby families gathered around their pianos over Christmas, although I rather doubt it.

My own earliest memories of Boxing Day at Depot Street are blurred by the effects of the obligatory lunchtime visit with Pat's father and uncle to a pub called the Douglas Bar on Normanton Road. Everyone referred to the pub as 'Harry Leonard's' because it had once been run by a footballer of that name who had played for Derby County before the First World War. My first visit there would be Boxing Day 1962, six days after my eighteenth birthday. Five pints of Bass later, I came tottering back to Depot Street, trying to disguise the fact that I was having difficulty standing up. I ate my lunch in silence and then dozed off beside the fire until teatime. If anyone noticed, they were kind enough not to mention it. Boxing Day lunchtimes at Harry Leonard's were apparently a family tradition (in the Buckler family that is, not the Poyntons; Pat's father never tired of telling the story of his teetotal wedding reception) but occasionally the ritual was moved to the Crystal Palace in Rosehill Street. By then I'd learned to pace myself, not least because if Derby County had a home fixture at the nearby Baseball Ground, going to the match with a bladderful of cold beer on a midwinter's afternoon was not a wise course of action.

Pat worked at the Co-op. After the 'Rochdale Pioneers', Derby's had been the second co-operative society in the world. Almost every family in Derby seemed to have a 'divi' number and it's still a party piece for many people to proudly recite it. The idea was that you gave the number every time you bought something and then, perhaps twice a year, the Co-op would declare a dividend for its members, who would queue at the offices in Albion Street to collect their money. Sometimes the Co-op dividend could be as much as 2s 6d in the pound, a return of 12½ per cent; compare that with the so-called store loyalty cards of today. Derby Co-op was a veritable empire. It seemed as if every neighbourhood had a Co-op grocery as well as a butcher's and a baker's shop. At one time there were as many as sixty such shops dotted around the town. The Co-op's main store in the town centre, in Exchange Street, sold everything from groceries and clothing to furniture and electrical goods. The Co-op had its own dairy (the illuminated Co-op Cow became an iconic feature, welcoming home Derbeians as their train drew towards Derby Midland station), building department, bakery, coal delivery business, undertakers, even a blacksmith's shop, and a garage to service its fleet of delivery vehicles. People could have their houses painted and decorated by the Co-op, which could also arrange holidays. When we were married, the Co-op provided the cars, so I've always told people that I had a society wedding. Pat's job was in the ladies' underwear department which was at the bottom of East Street, just before the old Castle and Falcon pub which stood on the corner of the Morledge. It was a fairly new development; a few years earlier I'd been one of the many Derbeians who'd stopped to peer through a hole in the high wooden fence that surrounded the demolition of the old shops, wondering what would take its place. Now I'd hover outside the underwear shop each evening, waiting for Pat to finish work while trying not to act like some kind of pervert who was lurking about to leer at ladies' corsets. On one occasion, the shop held a fashion parade in its window and the police had to be called when traffic ground to a halt as male motorists gawped at young women wearing nighties; the affair made the following day's *News of the World*, much to the distress of those taking part in what was a harmless bit of fun.

In the early 1960s, the complexion of Derby's shopping centre was significantly different from that of the twenty-first century. The area of today's brand-new Westfield Centre was then just a rabbit warren of narrow streets, while the main shopping thoroughfares were East Street, St Peter's Street, Victoria Street, Sadler Gate and the Cornmarket, with a few of the posher shops in Irongate. Those streets are still thriving today, but over forty years ago streets like Green Lane and the Wardwick were also buzzing with shoppers. Today, they are suffering as Derby's main shopping centre is being pulled to the south of the city. One of Derby's favourite department stores was the Midland Drapery on the corner of East Street and St Peter's Street; in fact, it occupied quite a sizeable chunk of both streets. The Midland Drapery was notable for the giant magnet which looked down on St Peter's Street, and also for its Christmas grotto in the basement. Several shops boasted grottoes with the regulation Santa Claus in attendance, but the Midland Drapery's seemed to be everyone's favourite. This was Derby's first department store, opened in 1892, and there were few Derbeians who didn't mourn its passing when it was closed in 1971 for redevelopment as a series of smaller shops that was to include the dreary Audley Centre. Part of the charm of the old Midland Drapery was the staff quarters on the top floor, where young female shop assistants lived after coming into the town from the surrounding countryside to work.

Another store that I thoroughly enjoyed visiting was Woolworth's in Victoria Street, if only for its wooden escalator and its weighing machine which produced a ticket with your weight stamped on it. By the middle of the 1950s I had begun to take an interest in popular music, and Woolworth's produced their own cover versions of hit parade favourites. Not that I ever bought any because I had nothing on which to play them. Our only entertainment came from a radio, rented from Telefusion in Babington Lane. In fact, this wasn't a wireless set at all, not in the sense that you could tune it in. It was simply a loudspeaker with a switch on the wall to alternate between whatever Telefusion chose to pipe through their system, usually the Light Programme, the Midland Home Service and the Third Programme. The Light Programme featured all the comedy shows, while the regional Home Service broadcast plays and programmes like the *Brains Trust* and *Round Britain Quiz*; the Third Programme was for those lovers of serious music who could afford the time to sit through Wagner's entire *Ring* cycle. For a few months, Telefusion experimented with Radio Luxembourg, so I became acquainted with the idea of commercially

Derby's famous Rolls-Royce band in concert. Trevor Poynton is unconventionally dressed because he has just done an impression of the cartoon character Andy Capp. (Author's Collection)

With wife Pat at the launch of the BBC Radio Derby series, 'The Derby County Story', which I wrote, in 1984. (Neil Simpson)

sponsored radio programmes, and I met the Ovaltinies, on air at least. Remember, though, this was still the mid-1950s and even on Radio Luxembourg the staple diet was David Whitfield, John Hanson, Guy Mitchell and Frankie Lane. Just occasionally, Elvis, or Bill Haley and his Comets, would butt in. The world as I knew it was about to change and by the time I left Bemrose School, that change was well under way.

Pleasures, though, were still relatively simple. If we weren't playing records in the front room at Depot Street, Pat and I would go for a walk. Of course, we aren't talking country lanes here because neither of us lived in what could remotely be described as a rural area. The nearest trees to Depot Street were in the nearby Arboretum, where, on Sunday afternoons, brass band concerts (sometimes featuring the Rolls-Royce band with Uncle Trevor among its number) drew large crowds. Otherwise it was a stroll on to Normanton Park, or sometimes, on our day off, a visit to Normanton Barracks to watch the Sherwood Foresters' regimental team play in the Derby and District Wednesday League; I was fortunate that my new girlfriend enjoyed football (and cricket) as much as I did. The Wednesday League catered for shop workers – on Wednesdays most town-centre businesses closed at lunchtime – who played for teams such as Market Hall, Derby Butchers and the Co-op, although Derby Post Office, Derby Borough Police, Derby Fire Brigade and the various Army regiments stationed around Derby also fielded sides. Sometimes we'd set off and perhaps walk around the ring road to Markeaton Park, or through the town to Darley Park. Most weeks we went to the cinema, although on the one occasion I persuaded Pat to go to the pictures on a Sunday teatime I had to swear a solemn oath not to let on to her mum who frowned upon such practices being undertaken on the Sabbath: in many older people's eyes, two seats on the back row of the Regal of a Sunday equated to eternal damnation. That was fair enough because our parents' parents were Victorians and those values had been ingrained in their children too. In the meantime, I had a train to catch.

CHAPTER TEN

Meeting Tony Curtis

In late July 1961 I answered an advertisement for what I thought was a summer holiday job at W.H. Smith's railway bookstall on Derby Midland station. With school behind me and with no real guidance or strong inclination as to what I wanted out of life, other than a feeling that it ought to be something to do with writing, I thought that at least I'd better start to earn some money. Stuart Clay, who had been accepted as a police cadet and was waiting to start his new job, walked down with me to the bookstall on a sunny Wednesday morning. Stuart hung around outside while I went into the small room at the end of the stall to be interviewed by the manager, a man called Laurence Alton. Loggy, as I was later to discover everyone called him, was a strange shape. He was fat and relatively small in height, standing perhaps 5ft 6in; at the very least, he looked almost as wide as he was tall. He was also round-shouldered and wore a navy blue suit, the lapels of which were covered with a thin dusting of cigarette ash. A pair of braces hoisted his trousers up almost to his armpits, and upon his ample stomach you could have placed a full pint of ale in the certain knowledge that not one drop would be spilt from that steady perch. He smelt of chips, stale tobacco and beer, and now he lit a John Player's Navy Cut, blew smoke over me, mopped his brow with a freshly pressed handkerchief and then sank wearily into the room's only chair while I stood uneasily against a packing bench.

He asked my full name, date of birth, school details, and then threw in a surprise: what were my hopes? Where did I see myself in ten years' time? I was completely thrown. I was only sixteen. Ten years was the best part of another lifetime away. I hadn't even thought about where I might be in a month's time. It certainly seemed an odd question to ask someone who had just turned up for a few weeks' pocket money. Quite why he was taking such an interest in my future, I couldn't imagine. Then the penny dropped. This was no mere holiday job. This was the real thing. I obviously hadn't read the advertisement properly. Or at least it hadn't made it clear that this was a full-time position, in which case I almost certainly wouldn't have applied for it. But whoever's fault it was, I knew that it would clearly be embarrassing for both of us to cut things short there and then. I decided to run with it. Newspapers, I said. Newspapers and magazines. And books. I'd always wanted to work with newspapers, magazines and books. And what better place than W.H. Smith's? Loggy seemed pleased. He coughed and some more cigarette ash tumbled down his waistcoat. He had always worked for W.H. Smith's, he said, apart from

W.H. Smith's bookstall at Derby Midland station, where I reported for duty in July 1961. (W.H. Smith Archive)

doing his bit in the Army during the war. I studied him again. If he really had been in the Army, then either Britain must have been truly desperate back in 1940, or here was a supreme example of a man who had let himself go to seed. He was from Derby, he said, but had worked mostly in Lincolnshire. That gave me a peg because, of course, my father came from the fens. So we chatted for a while about places we both knew. Eventually, we came back to the matter in hand. If I wanted it, he said, the job was mine. Four pounds a week with the prospect of rapid advancement as a relief manager once I'd learned the ropes. I had absolutely no intention of spending the rest of my life on a railway bookstall but, for now, what had I got to lose? I would have a job while I looked round for something better. We shook hands and I said that I could start on the following Monday (Derbyshire had just begun a three-day match against Warwickshire at the County Ground, and I had plans for the immediate future). That was OK, said Loggy, opening the door to the stall itself, where a bespectacled middle-aged woman and a youth were chatting in between serving customers.

'Bill', he called out. 'This is Anton. He's joining us next week.' I expected the youth to answer, but instead it was the woman who came over. She was Bill. She was also Mrs Alton, Loggy's wife. I never did find out why he called her Bill; maybe her name was Wilhelmina. The youth, it turned out, was a former carpet fitter called Tony Curtis, who had started at WHS a few weeks earlier. Introductions over, and with space at a premium in the small stall, there was nothing else for me to do but bid them farewell for now. In any case, I'd left Stuart waiting outside for the best part of an hour.

'See you on Monday then', I said.

'Yes,' said Loggy. 'Five-thirty sharp.'

That stopped me in my tracks. Five-thirty sharp? My heart fell. I was going to have to work evenings.

'Oh, I'm sorry', I said. 'I thought I was going to be working in the daytime.'

'That's right', said Loggy. 'You start at five-thirty in the morning. Till six.' Then, to make absolutely sure that I knew what I was in for, he added, 'Six in the evening.'

Maths had never been my strong point but the numerical fog lifted sufficiently for me to realise that this would be a twelve-and-a-half-hour day, something else for which I hadn't bargained. One minute I was applying for a nice little holiday job. The next I was being signed up for life and, by the looks of it, expected to sleep on the premises as well. I was soon wondering how I could hand in my notice before I'd even started. Maybe the best thing would be just to say cheerio for now, and then sneak back after they'd closed and post my resignation through the letter box. Yes, that's what I'd do. Walking back down Siddals Road, Stuart and I worked out the hourly rate. In 1961, they hadn't invented the minimum wage but, even then, just under 1s 3d an hour sounded like slave labour. Then came a change in the way we were thinking.

'I know', said Stuart, 'there must be overtime. Four pounds must be the flat rate. You know, for a forty-hour week or something. Then you'll rake it in, working all those hours.'

Getting up at 4.30 in the morning still seemed an extremely unappealing thing to do, but if there was more money in it. . . . Based on this assessment from a budding trainee police officer, I offered to treat Stuart to a game of snooker at the Regent before the cricket. Then I obviously needed to get some sleep.

And so, on Monday, 24 July 1961, at just after five in the morning, I found myself walking (with my eyes still partly shut) down Bradshaw Street, the little thoroughfare that linked Normanton Road to Osmaston Road. A few years later, Bradshaw Street would be swept away to be replaced by the much wider Bradshaw Way, another part of the jigsaw that was Derby's long-awaited inner ring road. For now, though, it was a tight little street and, most important, halfway down there was a gents' toilet. Two large cups of tea so early in the morning was already having an effect on my bladder. Indeed, over the next two years I was to become a regular patron of that gents' which often proved a life-saver on cold winter mornings. Pleasantly relieved, I arrived at the bookstall a few minutes before the appointed time – throughout my life I've always been early – to find it shuttered and bolted. A couple of railway porters were hanging about, but there was no sign of Loggy, or Bill, or the youth with the name of a famous film actor. It was Tony Curtis who arrived first, climbing off his bicycle in the station forecourt and then pushing it up to where I was waiting. He lived on Raynesway and cycled in every morning. We'd just begun to exchange small talk when a black Hillman Minx came slowly down Midland Road. It was Loggy and Bill.

And so began my two years at W.H. Smith's, during which time, incidentally, I was never paid a penny in overtime, despite what PC Clay had deduced. The hours were as stated, except on Saturdays when Tony and I could leave at 1 p.m. So, taking into account lunch breaks of an hour each day, that made it a 65-hour week, for £4 (actually, £3 13s 3d after deductions). Even getting on for half a century ago, I doubt it was legal for a sixteen-year-old (Tony was a year older) to work a 65-hour week. Not only that, we never actually knew the amount we were signing for when we drew our wages. It was Smith's custom to pay us in cash each Friday and, individually, we'd be called into the tiny office, no bigger than a telephone box, where Loggy would hand over the notes and coins – all loose, no wage packet – and then open up a ledger, the only visible part of which was the space for our signatures. Some months later, Tony found that Loggy had forgotten to lock his desk when he went for his lunchtime beer at the York Hotel opposite the station. My workmate pulled out the ledger and we began to scour the entries. There was a scam all right, but it wasn't that we were down for more than we were being paid. Instead there were listed several non-existent part-time employees. They were all drawing amounts just under the threshold for income tax or national insurance, so they were effectively falling through the government net. But collectively these phantom bookstall workers were earning enough for Loggy to almost double his salary. We put the ledger back where we'd found it. The matter had nothing to do with us.

Besides Loggy and Bill, Tony and me, there were four other flesh and blood employees. Mabel Blood, a lovely lady who originally came from Ashbourne but who now lived in Normanton, took over from Bill in the afternoons. She was a smashing person, always ready to help Tony and me if she could. Mrs Brown worked on the sub-stall on platform 1. She and her husband were big supporters of Derby Engineers' Club on Osmaston Road and, I believe, eventually became steward and stewardess there. Over on platform 6, Smith's ran a trolley which a little woman called Rhoda, who lived in Arthur Street near the Children's Hospital, pushed up and down whenever a train pulled in. Finally, we had a paper boy. In the late nineteenth and early twentieth centuries, when W.H. Smith & Son was *the* newsagent, all the big houses around the station and beyond had their newspapers delivered from the bookstall. Over the years, of course, many more neighbourhood newsagents had sprung up, while the occupants of those houses had died and habits had changed. There were, however, a handful of 'posher' households who clung to this tradition and the Derby stall still delivered a few papers as far afield as St Chad's Road and Mount Carmel Street. This is where Bill George came in, except that when I say he was our paper boy, that is using the term in its widest sense: Bill was well into his seventies. He was also one of the most colourful characters I'd ever met. For a start, I wasn't used to adults swearing. True, my father – and Loggy – would come out with the occasional 'bloody' or 'bugger', but Bill George was something else. Almost every other word was a four-letter one of Anglo-Saxon origin. He was in a permanently bad mood and each morning would come storming into the little stockroom, hurl his paperbag on to the packing bench, and then produce a foul-mouthed tirade against bad drivers, the weather, Harold Macmillan's Tory government, even Loggy and his wife. In fact, especially against Loggy and his wife. He did it to their faces, too, and they just took it all. And when Bill, who had seen action with the Coldstream Guards in Flanders during the First World War, had slammed the door and disappeared down Midland Road still muttering obscenities, they simply reflected on what a wonderfully rough diamond he was, to be sure. Yet Bill seemed to like Tony and me, and I grew quite fond of him because he made me roar with laughter every time he began ranting and raving.

Bill George was just one of a number of memorable characters who worked in and around the Midland station during the early 1960s. Chippy Wood, the gents' toilet attendant on platform 1, was a giant of a man with a big nose and a deep voice, who had also fought in the First World War. Chippy had a fund of colourful stories, mostly centring on his experiences in various French and Belgian brothels during the years 1914 to 1918. The one thing for which Chippy could always be relied on was a mug of steaming hot tea on a cold winter's morning. Loggy had banned the mashing of tea in the stall itself because of the mess. Apparently dirty cups and saucers were always being left for Mrs Alton to wash up, so one day, in a rage, he'd thrown them, and the kettle and teapot, into a dustbin. From the day I arrived, we always had to buy our tea from the railway buffet, although we were allowed a discount if we told the assistant 'OCS', which meant 'on company's service', a relic of the days before nationalisation when the Midland Railway Company ran the station. Another source of tea was Chippy's counterpart in the ladies' toilet. A large woman with dyed jet-black hair and a heavily made-up complexion, May (I never knew her surname) would mash the strongest tea I'd ever seen. In colour it wavered between bright orange and sludge; it needed several spoonsful of sugar; and even then it could make a strong man shudder. But like Chippy, May possessed a heart of gold. In fact, most of the people who worked down there were thoroughly nice individuals. I got on particularly well with a red-haired chap called John, whose job it was to sell tea and refreshments off a trolley which he pushed up and down standing trains before they continued their journey. John, whose wife, Kora, was Dutch, came from Spalding which, of course, I knew well, and so we had plenty to chat about.

For Tony and me, duties were varied. First thing in the morning we had to collect all the newspapers and magazines from the parcels office, then stock the counter and make up Bill George's paper round. We also had to make up a round for the station itself before delivering publications like *The Engineer* to people like the British Railways' chief mechanical and electrical engineer who was based in the myriad of offices. There was a strict hierarchy at the Midland station. At its head was the stationmaster, the omnipotent Mr Gilmour who always wore a bowler hat and a pin-striped suit; except, that is, when VIPs were passing through, in which case he would don full morning dress, top hat and all. His son Bruce later worked with John Cheadle at the Co-op Travel and became one of our regular drinking chums. By VIPs, I mean members of the royal family and the government. Mr Gilmour wasn't going to get out his topper for the likes of Cliff Richard, to whom I once sold a *Daily Sketch*, or the world middleweight boxing champion Terry Downes, who once bought from me a copy of *World Sports*. One character who did irritate me was a man who was allowed to borrow magazines for nothing. He'd worked in the railway offices since before the war and still took advantage of a perk that should surely have been dumped years earlier. He sported a waxed moustache, wore a bowler hat and a regimental tie (I think he still clung to some military title), and carried a rolled umbrella. Every Friday, on his way home, he collected just about every available magazine and then returned them, creased and covered in stains and bits of dried food, the following Wednesday. It was, however, his manner that annoyed me most. He treated the rest of us like servants. I'd always been brought up to respect everybody, no matter what job they did, so I regarded this chap as simply ignorant.

When we'd finished sorting out and delivering the day's newspapers and magazines, Tony and I had to clear everything up and dispose of the rubbish. This involved fetching a goods porter's barrow, loading it with all the string and wrapping, and then wheeling it down platform 1 and across the main lines that connected the north of Britain with the south. Our destination was an incinerator under London Road bridge, where we burned everything. It was a truly hazardous operation and, quite rightly, wouldn't be allowed today. To begin with, we had no idea when a train was likely to come steaming into the station, so we literally took our lives in our hands as we dashed across the tracks, bouncing the barrow behind us. Sometimes one of its wheels would become stuck in the lines and one of us would have to work feverishly to free it while the other kept an eye out for the London express or 'The Devonian' as it roared into Derby. On days when visibility was down to a few feet, this proved particularly nerve-racking, especially if a fog detonator suddenly exploded nearby. The station was a filthy place to work because steam engines still operated – one or two diesels were just being introduced – and there was always smoke and soot everywhere. Yet these were also happy times and the pair of us enjoyed exploring the complex. One day, we were wandering along a loading dock at the end of platform 1 when Tony stuck his head inside a goods carriage to discover that it contained a coffin. We climbed in to investigate and decided to pick it up. Tony got hold of one end, I got hold of the other, and together we began to lift the casket off its trestle. We thought it would be empty, but the realisation that it must have contained a body dawned on us both at exactly the same time. We dropped the coffin simultaneously, jumped back through the carriage door and fled down the platform. It was some days before we ventured up to that end of the station again. Life at W.H. Smith's also served up my most embarrassing moment to date. Walking down Carrington Street one day, after delivering a magazine to a railway office there, I swung my foot at a stone, only for my shoe to fly off. I watched in horror as it described an arc and, with perfect geometry, disappeared through the open window of the GPO sorting office. Red-faced, I had to limp through the door (well, one foot was now higher than the other) and ask for my shoe back. It took them some time to locate it, during which I had to endure plenty of leg-pulling: at one point it was suggested that the shoe had landed on a conveyor belt and was now irreversibly on its way to Manchester, first-class recorded.

For me, however, all this jolly larking about was about to stop, and at the worst possible time, too. In November 1962 it started getting unseasonably cold as temperatures fell steadily all over Britain. In December came what turned out to be the last of the old-style smogs, when a combination

The back room of the bookstall. I am waiting to undertake another life-or-death trip to the incinerator. (Tony Curtis)

of domestic coal smoke and sulphur dioxide products created acidic fog droplets which, in turn, caused major respiratory problems that were to kill many elderly people that winter. The cold spell persisted through January and February and into early March with continuous sub-zero temperatures, making it the coldest winter over England and Wales since 1740. In January, the mercury in the Midlands dropped to a record low and there it remained, which meant that the frequent severe snowfalls, which had begun on Boxing Day, never cleared away before the next lot arrived, and so thick snow remained on the ground until Easter was in sight. The sea even froze for some distance off the Kent coast.

So this was not a good time for me to be sent on my travels. My 'apprenticeship' over, W.H. Smith decided that it was time for me to spread my wings; they sent me on relief work to Loughborough, in Leicestershire. On the face of it, it was a good move because it meant working in a High Street shop rather than on a cold, draughty railway bookstall. The downside was having to travel by train each day during one of the most dreadful winters that anyone could remember. Getting there each morning was, ironically, easy enough. The London train never seemed to be late. Getting home at night was an entirely different matter. Trains coming north were hours late and the homeward journey also involved a change of train at a station in the middle of nowhere, called Trent. Night after night I'd find myself sitting shivering on a porter's barrow at Trent, with no-one for company, waiting for a train to Derby to come creeping out of the fog. I'd arrive back at the Midland station at getting on for 10 p.m., walk home to Gerard Street through the freezing fog, sliding around on icy pavements as I went, and then set off again well before dawn to repeat the whole horrible process. I have never been so utterly miserable in my entire life. One December night, taking a detour from the station through Derby Arboretum to see Pat in Depot Street, I found the fog so thick that I was completely disoriented. I literally couldn't see my hand in front of my face. Then suddenly I bumped into some railings and realised that I'd collided with the Arboretum's fountain. From there I knew the layout of the park and, twenty minutes later (it would have taken less than five in good visibility), I was ringing the doorbell at Pat's house.

By Easter, which fell right at the end of March that year, the worst of the weather was over and, with impeccable timing, Smith's recalled me from Loughborough. For four months I'd travelled there six days a week, through fog, snow and ice, sitting alone on bleak railway platforms waiting in the dark for trains that never came. Now the days were getting longer and the weather was improving, the company had decided to bring me back to base. The summer of 1963 dragged on and Tony and I sent for a book we'd seen advertised in the weekly *Reveille* magazine. It was called *101 Ways To Be Your Own Boss* and cost 2s 6d plus post and packing. Maybe we could set something up together to escape long hours spent on a grimy railway station. When the book arrived we eagerly tore open the wrapping and flicked through the pages. It was a home-made affair that looked as if it had been bound on someone's mother's sewing machine, in a back room with the police knocking on the door. Ways to be your own boss included garaging bicycles on match days (possible, if you happened to live near a football ground) and clearing snow from garden paths (which, in the winter just gone, would actually have been a money-spinner). Alas, there was no serious business plan anywhere in the book which was a complete rip-off. Actually, the one good idea was missing: advertise a book showing you 101 ways to become your own boss, and then sit back as the half-crowns came rolling in from mugs like us.

With this entrepreneurial setback, things were becoming desperate. As the nights began to draw in again, I was told that I was being moved to Gainsborough, in Lincolnshire. I wasn't going to get there and back in a day; I would have to find digs. That was the final straw: I'd been going out with Pat for eighteen months now and didn't see how that was going to work if I was living permanently 62 miles away; and all my friends were in Derby, where I was heavily involved in local football. If I'd had the slightest intention of pursuing a career with W.H. Smith then I might have worked something out, but I'd remained with them far too long as it was, letting my life drift along. That night I saw an advertisement for a job in a shop that was opening in Derby's new Main Centre precinct, off London Road. King's Agencies was a London-based chain of newsagents and record shops. Anything would do in order to save me from Gainsborough. I dashed off an application just before I went on holiday with Stuart Clay, to Scarborough to watch the cricket festival. When I returned a week later, there was a letter waiting for me, asking me to go for an interview. It was conducted at a private house at Maine Drive, Chaddesden, where the new shop's manager, Trevor Middleton, lived. He gave me the job on the spot, and the following day I went into Loggy's little office to hand in my notice. I was expecting him to say how sorry he was to lose me. He didn't, and he obviously wasn't.

'Righto', he said, without looking up from fiddling the wages ledger, 'when are you leaving?'

'Next week, if that's OK', I said. He didn't reply, so I assumed it was OK. A few days later, I went with Tony up to the George Hotel on Midland Road, where we had a farewell drink. He had been a grand workmate and I was sorry to part company with him. In fact, Tony stayed on at the bookstall, was made manager after Loggy retired, saw the stall demolished and resited, not once but twice, and was still working there in 2007, so I still saw him whenever I caught a train from Derby. In the mid-1970s, he even asked me to be the best man at his wedding. I was going to tell the story about the coffin until Pat kicked me on the shins and reminded me that it wasn't the sort of tale you recounted at a wedding reception.

Of course, the job at King's Agencies turned out to be every bit the dead-end post that I'd anticipated, although I did meet Gene Pitney, Ronnie Carroll, Cathy McGowan and the group Manfred Mann, all of whom were appearing in Derby and did some promotional appearances at the Main Centre. When the company needed a relief manager, it also involved me living in a flat in Walsall (why were people so keen for me to leave Derby?). A few weeks later, I answered an advertisement for a job at the *Derby Evening Telegraph*.

Smith's bookstall in the 1970s, long after I'd left but looking much the same as in the days when I shivered there before dawn. Only the fashions have changed. (Derby Evening Telegraph)

CHAPTER ELEVEN

They Shouldn't Count Goals Like That

It was the early autumn of 1959 and we needed a name for our new football club. Walking back up Abbey Street, on our way from Bemrose School, the remnants of the gang that had trailed homewards down Drewry Lane passed a cobbler's shop. In the window was an advertisement for Redfern Rubbers, a well-known shoe sole. So, for no other reason than that, the title of what was to become one of Derby's best-known local football clubs was established. Later that month, Redfern Athletic played its first match against a scratch team on Rykneld Recreation Ground. I can't remember the exact score but we won by six or seven goals. I managed to get one of them, a humping, hopeful wallop, vaguely in the direction of goal, from about 40yd. The ball bounced once on the rock-hard pitch (1959 had been a scorching summer), their goalkeeper came out yards too far, and the leather sailed over his head and bobbled gently over the line. No-one came to congratulate me. 'They shouldn't count goals like that', snorted Stuart Clay, who went on to score three good ones that day. For the next twenty years, Redfern Athletic provided me – and dozens of others – with a social life that far exceeded the simple pleasure of playing football. Getting on for half a century later, many aspects of our lives had faded into distant memory. Except for Redfern Athletic. Several former colleagues were still old friends. Others I bumped into now and again. And occasionally, someone who I didn't even recognise would come up wanting to talk about the time they played for Redfern.

In those formative years, we played only friendly matches because we wanted to play on Sundays and football on the Sabbath was banned by the Football Association, which was a pity because the standard was higher than many of the bona fide Saturday leagues that flourished all over Britain. In Derby alone there were hundreds of Saturday clubs; each weekend every pitch on the old Derby Racecourse and on Darley Fields was in use. They were no good to us, however, because we watched Derby County every other Saturday, so Sunday football gave us the opportunity to both watch and play. For obvious reasons, local opponents weren't always easy to find and so we travelled – to Sheffield, Birmingham and Manchester, anywhere within a day's march where we could find decent opposition and a pub conveniently reopening as we neared home again.

Redfern Athletic in 1960. Back row, left to right: me, Terry King, Stuart Clay, Peter Handford, Arthur Auger, Norman Saxon. Front row: Trevor Smith, Hedley Mayze, John Cheadle, Paddy Donnelly, Barry Iremonger. (Author's Collection)

Despite its being illegal, at least so far as the FA was concerned, Sunday football flourished in many big cities, where top Saturday players turned out under false names. Facilities, however, varied considerably and some council parks departments locked and barred their dressing-rooms on Sundays, which meant that changing beside a hedgerow, and then using a pitch without actually paying for it, was not all that unusual. There were some surprises along the way. In the dreadful winter of 1962/3, we arranged a match against Sheffield Antiques FC, a club which was made up of local university students. When we arrived at the original venue, it was under a snowdrift and we were escorted to another pitch. There were still about six inches of snow on that and, to make matters worse, there was a tree stump at outside-right; I wouldn't have minded, but I kept losing the ball to it.

Manchester was a regular venue, and in the days when the M6 motorway was still on the drawing board, this usually meant a long but pleasant journey north through Derbyshire. We always timed our return so that we'd be pulling up at the Talbot in Belper just as the landlord, the former Derby County outside-left, Jack Robson, was unbolting the front door of his pub. A couple of pints and a game of darts and we'd be on our way again. Playing in Manchester often took us into some dodgy areas. One game, against North Hulme Celtic at Hulme Barracks, was in a particularly run-down part of the city and we were glad to find all our possessions still intact when we returned to the dressing-room. My memory is of a rock-hard pitch set among towering blocks of those high-rise flats that were mushrooming all over Britain in the early 1960s. I was surprised to discover recently that Hulme Barracks is now a Grade II listed building. I bet there's no blue plaque to say that Redfern Athletic once played there. After games in Manchester we'd make our way into the city centre, grab a plate of egg and chips and then pile into the Manchester News Theatre which was opposite the Odeon in Oxford Street. This tiny cinema showed a collection of cartoons and newsreels in a programme that lasted for about an hour and ran continuously from 10 a.m. At ninepence in old money it was good value. Stuart Clay perfected his Woody Woodpecker impression in that very venue. Then there would be the usual happy coach journey back to Derby, with a few rousing choruses of the Temperance Seven favourite, 'Pasadena', or, unless we could stop him, a maudlin rendition by Trevor McCandless of Elvis Presley's 'Old Shep'. Our star player at this time was a quiet lad called Ian Becket, who'd been capped for the England youth team. I can see him now, chuckling away to himself at the back of the bus.

Trevor Mac was one of a new generation of Redfern players. My old Bemrose School pals, John Cheadle, Stuart Clay and Malc Spare were regulars in the team, and other Old Bemrosians, like Trevor, signed up as they left school. Keri Haywood was a blond-haired outside-left, generally known as 'Snowy' but occasionally as 'The Colonel'. When we began to run a cricket team, we called it Colonel Haywood's XI, which at least impressed opponents. Keri was on the small side but he was a hard little player who took knocks from big defenders and never flinched. One day, after a match in Leicester, a man in a long raincoat came up and, claiming that he was a scout for Arsenal, asked Keri for his name and address. As far as I know, Keri never heard from Highbury, and the general consensus was the man in the mac just liked him, although if he did get in touch, Keri never let on. An accountant, Keri worked for Fletcher & Stewart Ltd, the Derby-based makers of sugar refinery equipment, before he set up his own engineering business. Alas, through no fault of his own, things eventually went wrong there and he took it badly. He was a good, honest friend and it was sad that, after his company went under, he didn't feel able to join in with his old pals any more, although he did get deeply involved with Matlock Cricket Club, where his son, Matthew, played. It was a great upset when Keri died in August 2001; he was only fifty-four and it seemed like only yesterday that he was dodging a hefty right-back, or joining in with some daft jape or other.

Keri's Bemrose contemporaries who became Redfern regulars included Peter Shone, who went on to play semi-professionally for Burton Albion in the Southern League, Alan Dobson, Paul Walton, Ian Browning and Sid Sharp, who was our regular goalkeeper for many years. I got on with Sid particularly well and he was my room-mate when we played abroad. It was much closer to home, however, that he was confronted with a situation that can't have tested many goalkeepers, amateur or professional, over the years. We were playing up in Lancashire, against Bury North End. There is still a club of this name today but it appears to be no relation to the outfit we were unfortunate enough to meet well over forty years ago. It was a miserable day, pouring with rain, the pitch waterlogged. The first thing of note that happened was that the referee's watch stopped and he borrowed one from a spectator. A few moments later, the ref sent off one of our players. This proved a complication: it turned out that the borrowed watch was his; a non-playing member of our party had been looking after it. Before he would leave the field, our player demanded the return of his watch from the official and the game was held up for several minutes while a replacement timepiece was found. At half-time we were winning 2–0, but as we lined up for the second half, the Bury centre-forward strolled into the goalmouth we were now defending and proceeded to urinate in a puddle. 'I bet you won't want to dive in that,' he told an astonished Sid Sharp. Fortunately, Sid didn't have to as we kept them at bay and even added a third goal before the end. We normally had a cup of tea with the opposition, but on this occasion we were straight on the bus and soon on the road back to Derby, via the Talbot at Belper, of course.

Unsurprisingly, there was also a brush with some unpleasant characters when we played against a team of long-term prisoners at Nottingham prison. About fifteen minutes from the end, their centre-forward, who was about forty and claimed that he'd once played professionally for Cardiff City, elbowed me smack on the nose. Bloodied, I was taken to the prison medical wing where a warder with some first-aid training stuffed cotton

Trooping off after a charity match against an ex-Derby County XI at Littleover in April 1964. I am on the extreme left, walking off behind Arnie Grace, Tommy Powell, Derek Taylor, Ken Oliver and Tim Ward, who was the Rams manager at the time. (Tony Curtis)

wool up my nose, said he thought it was broken, and told me to go to hospital once we were back in Derby. A couple of weeks earlier, I'd sat through a horror story when someone on an opposing team told how he'd broken his nose and a doctor at the Derbyshire Royal Infirmary had straightened it by pushing a pair of scissors (handles first, you'll be pleased to know) up his nostrils and then jerking the crooked hooter back into place, all without the aid of anaesthetic. When I got home, I gingerly removed the cotton wool, surveyed the damage in a mirror, decided it didn't look too bad and gave the DRI a miss. Despite the impromptu nose-job courtesy of a centre-forward doing a twelve-stretch for armed robbery, the one memory I have of being inside a prison is the smell: boiled cabbage and stale urine. It made me vow never to break the law.

Nottingham prison was just up the road but eventually we went further afield, playing end-of-the-season matches in Belgium. It became a regular tour, and it was the scene of my last appearance on a football pitch. By May 1965 Sunday football had been legalised for a couple of years and we had just finished our first season in the newly formed Derby Sunday League. Earlier that season, I'd been sent off after an altercation with a chap called Frank Nix during a game against Castle Sports on Darley Fields. There was nothing to it, just handbags at five paces. But fists were raised, blows swung (I can't remember if one actually landed), and the referee, Dave Storer, sent us both to the dressing room. A few weeks later we appeared before the Derbyshire FA's disciplinary panel at the York Hotel and were each fined 10s. I was never happy about amateur players being fined; I was earning only about £10 a week at the time and ten bob was a significant portion of that. About forty years later, I was enjoying a pint in the Captain Blake pub in Agard Street when a man came over. He was about my age, sported a crew-cut and looked as if he'd been around a bit, so when he demanded to know if I was Anton Rippon, my first reaction was to say, 'Depends'. It was Frank Nix. We shook hands and had a laugh about the day we were branded hooligans by the DFA secretary, Les Overton.

A few weeks after the sending-off incident, we were playing against Derby Law Clerks on the Racecourse when a lad called Colin Hilton caught me a fearful blow on the left ankle. It wasn't his fault; we'd both gone for the ball together and Colin just mistimed his kick, but he left me with a massive bruise with blood literally slopping about inside the injury. I'd never been a good player. I just relied on a philosophy of being happy to let either the ball or the opponent go past me – just never both at the same time. Now, for the rest of that season I was troubled by a red-hot stabbing pain every time I kicked the ball with my left foot (which, admittedly, wasn't all that often). The team was also improving and we were playing a higher standard of football. Eventually, I had to admit that there was now no room for a left-back whose only skill lay in dealing out gravel rash to foolhardy wingers. So, on an unseasonably bleak May Saturday afternoon, on the works pitch of a fish-canning factory in Ostend, against a team from the local tax office, my playing career came to an inglorious end. We drew 2–2, John Cheadle scored both our goals, and I limped out of football for ever. I can, however, say that the opposing goalkeeper in my last game of competitive soccer had played for Belgium against England in the 1954 World Cup. Talk about reflected glory.

Elaborate practical jokes had always been a highlight of Redfern Athletic. In the early summer of 1966, we managed to convince Derek Grantham, a useful full-back from Normanton who now lives in Melbourne, Australia, that he'd been chosen as a ball boy for the World Cup Final at Wembley that July. He changed his holidays in order to attend, and there was even an article about his forthcoming adventure in the International Combustion works newspaper. It really got out of hand and, in the end, we drew lots to see who would tell him it was all a joke. I lost but, happily, Derek was a good-natured soul and he saw the funny side of it; I was walking again in less than a fortnight. John Cheadle, though, was less than happy that we'd elected to come clean. When it came to taking the mickey, John was like a dog with a bone; he just wouldn't let go. 'Why spoil it now?' he complained. 'We could have got him all the way to Wembley.'

Released from these shores, of course the mickey-taking reached new heights. Our 1965 visit to Belgium was the first foreign trip for many of us. Colin Shaw kept missing mealtimes because Cheadle told him that Belgium was three hours ahead of the UK and so Colin spent the first day with his watch that much ahead of everyone else's before the penny dropped. Trevor

A Redfern trip to Ostend in 1967. Left to right are Linda Ward, John Cheadle, Christine Beeson, John Hudson, Janet McCandless, Trevor McCandless (with giant bottle), Marion Keeling, Jimmy Symcox, Dave Keeling and John Swanwick. (Author's Collection)

McCandless eagerly signed up for Cheadle's day-trip from Ostend to Rome by bus. And, together with Sid Sharp, I tried to batter to death a repulsive-looking lizard we found in our bedroom. It was a couple of minutes before we realised that it was made of plastic. Cheadle and Walton had placed it on our window sill, complete with a drop of water by its mouth. Well, we'd never been abroad before. We weren't even sure if you could drink the tap water, so why wouldn't there be a poisonous reptile lurking in a Belgian hotel bedroom? There were plenty of myths about foreign shores. Alas, the first to be dispelled was that continental morals were so lax that, on the other side of the English Channel, there were hundreds of loose women just waiting to have their wicked way with innocent young men from places like Derby. In the end we were happy enough to discover that there didn't appear to be any limit on foreigners' pub licensing hours.

Back home, the FA's decision to recognise Sunday football (there was now so much of it they it would have been impossible for them to continue to ignore it) had brought about the formation of the Derby Sunday League. The inaugural meeting at the Exchange Hotel next door to the *Evening Telegraph* offices was hysterically funny. The secretary of one new club was desperate to get his name recorded at this historic occasion. A well-built man with a thick neck and beady eyes, he ran a football club attached to a building firm. Every time someone proposed a motion, he shot up his hand but the chairman kept getting a seconder from elsewhere on the floor. Eventually, this chap kept his hand raised and yelled out in exasperation 'Well I'll third it then.' When the draw was made for the league knockout cup, I almost fell off my chair when the chairman drew a ball and announced, 'Number six', then peered at it again, and said, 'No, sorry, number nine.' The first few games were a bit odd as well. During one game on the Racecourse it began to rain heavily and, without first stopping play, the referee left the field to don a pacamac and a flat cap. 'What on earth are you doing?' I asked. 'I've had a cold all week', he explained.

Former Derby County part-time professional Pip Parr, whose father also played for the Rams, sees his shot blocked while playing for Redfern Athletic Reserves in a local cup final at the Municipal Sports Ground in the 1960s. Such games always attracted large crowds. (Author's Collection)

Redfern Athletic, 1970. Back row, left to right: Mick Camp (manager), Alan Dobson, Dave Connor, Dave Tretton, Jack Webb, Trevor McCandless, Ray Harrison. Front row: Les Haines, John Cheadle, Peter Shone, Steve Gibson, Stuart Woodings. (Author's Collection)

After my decision to give up trying to play football, I concentrated on being club secretary and saw Redfern march on to greater things. Success in the Derby league saw us move into the Midland Sunday League in which many semi-professionals played. We had to improve, too, and new signings were made. I was delighted when I persuaded my favourite Derby County player of all time, Tommy Powell, who had played over 400 games for the Rams, to join us along with other former Derby players like Nigel Cleevely and Ronnie Metcalf, both of whom had also played league football for the Rams. Mick Camp, father of Lee Camp who started 2006 as the Rams' goalkeeper, became our manager. Then Dave Agnew, who'd played for Notts County, took over as player-manager. Leading local players like Steve Buckley, who went on to play over 350 first-team games for Derby County, Steve Sibley and Stuart Woodings, a Rams Reserves midfielder, formed the backbone of an excellent team. Sid Sharp had now been posted out of Derby by the bank for which he worked, and his place was taken by Dave Tretton, yet another player on the Rams' books; Dave had been with us for only a short time when Brian Clough loaned him to League of Ireland club, Cork Hibernian. We became good friends and, like his predecessor in Redfern's goal, Dave was my roommate on a few foreign trips. Dave, who came from Allenton, went into the Civil Service and, the last I heard, was the chief ratings officer for the part of London that includes Buckingham Palace. Dave Tretton sending the Queen her rates bill? Actually, I don't think she has to pay any.

We began to run three teams and, at one stage, our reserve side included Peter Ward, who went on to play for Nottingham Forest, Brighton and England; Colin Tunnicliffe, who won a NatWest Trophy winners' medal as an all-round cricketer with Derbyshire; and three amateur footballers, each of whom became powerful players in television sport: Trevor East was responsible for negotiating the multi-million pound package between Sky TV and the Premier League; Vic Wakeling became managing director of Sky Sports; and Mark Sharman replaced Brian Barwick as controller of ITV sport when Barwick went off to become the Football Association's new chief executive. Trevor had worked for the Derby news agency, Raymonds, while both Vic and Mark were employed by the *Derby Evening Telegraph*. It seems strange now that each of these five young men running around a football field at Littleover in the early 1970s would one day enjoy such diverse but high-powered careers.

While we were still in the local Derby league, we scored a remarkable victory in the national competition, the FA Sunday Cup, beating Players Athletic No Names, the previous season's semi-finalists, before a 3,000-strong crowd at Aspley Lane, Nottingham. These were heady times for the club named after a brand of shoe sole. Four-figure attendances were also not unusual for our home games on the King George VI ground at Carlisle Avenue, Littleover, especially if it was a local derby against our great rivals, Northcliffe United. Redfern's annual dinners became legendary: 300 people packed the Pennine Hotel and then the Newton Park Hotel to hear speakers like comedians Cardew 'The Cad' Robinson and Dave King, and England bowler Fred Trueman, and to dance the night away to

In the 1950s, Cardew 'The Cad' Robinson was a famous radio comedian. By 1967, he wasn't famous at all, which is why we could afford him as an after-dinner speaker. The Cad is pictured here with John Cheadle. (Author's Collection)

local group, Rain. There were car rallies, cricket matches and ten-pin bowling nights, even an annual charity game in aid of the blind, against an ex-Rams team. I played in the first two of these and never quite overcame the experience of directly opposing little Reg Harrison who'd won an FA Cup winners' medal in the first postwar Final at Wembley. Reg was by now in his fortieth year and, in front of a large crowd at Carlisle Avenue, I had to abandon my normal approach to a tricky winger: kicking lumps out of a Derby County legend just didn't seem right, even supposing I could ever have caught up with him.

We also held a regular social evening at the Duke of York on Burton Road. The landlady let us have an upstairs room which had its own bar. We played darts, cards and generally chatted about that afternoon's match. New Year's Eve parties were held at the Norman Arms in Village Street, and we used the White Horse in the Morledge for drawing our weekly tote, which was then one of the biggest run by a local football club. When I was working for the *Derby Evening Telegraph* at Burton, our office pub was the Royal Oak in the Market Place. One of the landlords in my time was Tom Wencell, who discovered a large upstairs room in an outside building. Tom wanted to smarten it up and hold functions there and so I agreed to bring over a coachload of Redfern players and officials one evening. All went well until I was returning from the gents' toilet. The function room was reached by climbing a wooden outside staircase. I'd just got my foot on the bottom step when the door at the top was flung open and, bathed in a pool of electric light and a cloud of tobacco smoke, there swayed a figure holding a pint in one hand and a cigarette in the other. The figure began to negotiate the steps but, halfway down, he tumbled over and came crashing to my feet. I turned him over and, to my horror, saw the Trent Bus driver staring happily back at me.

When it was time to go home, he was obviously in no state to drive so we laid him on the back seat and wondered what to do next. Then up stepped one of our committeemen, Steve Verran, who announced that a friend he'd brought with him was the proud owner of a PSV (public service vehicle) licence. He would drive the bus back to Derby. And so he did. The only problem was that, because of a neck injury, Steve's pal was wearing a surgical collar and he could only look straight ahead; he couldn't turn his head left or right. Somehow we got back to Derby, despite almost getting the bus stuck under the low-level Moor Street railway bridge in Burton. Safely back home, we left the bus outside the Trent garage on Uttoxeter New Road and went our separate ways into the night, leaving the driver snoring peacefully on the back seat. We never did find out what happened to him. I hope he woke up in time to put the bus back in the garage and slip off home before anyone saw him.

Redfern Athletic was much more than just a football club. By the late 1970s, however, priorities were changing. The original players were hanging up their boots. People were married with growing families. And, where we had been pleased to walk miles for a game of football, young players now wanted the guarantee of a lift before they would consider playing for anyone. In 1977, with a new job and other distractions, I left the club, which carried on until the early 1980s before, like so many of the big names of local football, it too folded. Redfern went the way of Northcliffe United, Olympiads Sports and the like. And yet none of them really died. The spirit lives on, and it isn't often I walk through Derby without someone stopping me to ask, 'You used to run Redfern Athletic, didn't you?'

CHAPTER TWELVE
Gone for a Burton

In April 1965, I reported to the *Derby Evening Telegraph*'s office in the brewing town of Burton upon Trent, just over the Staffordshire border. Burton was eleven miles up the road from our house in Gerard Street and a town I already knew quite well; my father and I'd often caught the bus there to watch Burton Albion when they entertained attractive opposition, such as the time we saw the great Jackie Milburn playing in the Southern League after his career with Newcastle United and England had ended. Now I was back, and on the way to spending ten very happy years there, albeit it was originally intended that I should be sent there for only a few weeks to learn the ropes. It was also the start of a road that, with a few twists along the way, would take me into journalism.

The job was in the *Telegraph*'s publishing department whose primary responsibility was for the newspaper's circulation but whose role also took in running the satellite branch offices at places like Burton, Ripley and Ilkeston. The manager of the Burton office, Eddie Sephton, had been on long-term sick leave and after a few weeks it was decided that I could be left there unsupervised; after a few months, when Eddie decided that his health would be better served by working in Derby rather than travelling to Burton each day, they gave me his job. I'd quickly learned to type because one of my first jobs was to collate the racing results (and, on Saturdays, the football half-times and results) as well as late news that was either phoned through from Derby, or sent via the teleprinter that chattered away in the reporters' room in our small office on the corner of Abbey Arcade and the Market Place. After being typed on to a stencil, the late news and sports results were then printed into the stop press, or 'fudge', of copies of the *Telegraph* that had been produced in Derby and then delivered to us at about 2.30 p.m. each day.

The Burton office was a tight-knit operation which the chief reporter, a large, bearded man called Dave Stacey, continually livened up with his great bellowing laugh. When he wasn't out on a job – he rode a motor-cycle – or typing up his copy, Dave, who resembled the Bluto character from the Popeye cartoon, could usually be found holding court at the Royal Oak on the other side of the Market Place; he was a legendary figure in Burton. In those days, local football clubs like Burton Albion were covered by a news reporter from the branch office, whether he knew anything about football or not. As soon as Dave realised that the game was my number one passion, he offered me 7s 6d a week to write his football column for the Saturday night *Green 'Un*. It would have been money for old rope but I was pleased to do it for nothing more than a drink. It should be said that Dave was such a good operator that he'd already been doing the football column for years without readers ever spotting that he disliked the game intensely and knew little about it. He hardly needed me.

Another football-hating reporter who was at Burton when I arrived was John Orgill, who later became a Derby town councillor and whose wife, Lucy, for many years served as the *Evening Telegraph*'s women's editor and who continues to write a very popular weekly column in the paper. John was always up for a laugh and we played many a trick on the others. On one occasion he came across an unused Post Office telegram envelope and, with the aid of some copy paper and the right typewriter face, produced a authentic-looking telegram that read, 'Imperative you ignore earlier telegram.' We had a fussy receptionist called Elsie Goodall, and John addressed it to her, leaving it on her desk when she was at lunch. We thought that she'd just scratch her head and ask, 'What other telegram?' Unfortunately, we'd forgotten that her husband was a long-distance lorry driver. Mrs Goodall's imagination went into overdrive and it took some considerable effort to calm her down and explain that it was just a joke. She didn't see the funny side. In fact, I think that was the last day she ever made a cup of tea for any of us.

On another occasion we took Dave Stacey's motor-cycle crash helmet and suspended it from a hook in the very high ceiling of the reporters' room. To retrieve the helmet so that he could go out on a job, Dave had to drag a desk across the room, pile up a few of the bound volumes of back numbers that we kept, and then precariously balance on them to unhook his helmet. Unfortunately he was in a rare bad mood that day

John Orgill took this picture of me outside the Evening Telegraph *office in Burton in 1966. (Author's Collection)*

and, to make room on the desk for his high-wire act, he threw a typewriter on the floor. To our horror, the carriage shot straight off across the room. Damaging company property was obviously frowned upon, but Dave would have nothing to do with it. 'It's your fault for buggering about, so you can get it mended', he said as he stormed out. We found a typewriter repair shop near Burton Town Hall and showed the machine, now in two parts, to the proprietor. He scratched his head, disappeared into the back of the shop and returned several minutes later with a dog-eared catalogue. It turned out that the typewriter (they were usually passed to editorial only after accounts had finished with them) had been made in Leipzig some time before the First World War. It was irreparable, so we took it back and put it on an empty desk; it was still there, gathering dust, when I left seven years later.

For a while, John gave me a lift to work (actually he demanded my bus fare, although it was door-to-door service so I couldn't complain), but one Friday morning in December 1965 we struggled to get to Burton at all. The previous evening I'd gone with John Cheadle to see Swadlincote's heavyweight boxer, Jack Bodell, fight in what turned out to be the future British champion's only professional bout in his home county. Bodell took on the champion of Spain, Benito Canal, but the Spaniard looked neither fit nor interested, and the Derbyshire man soon stopped him. We left the King's Hall in Derby in disgust and went for a drink. It had been raining steadily for much of the day, but neither of us gave it much thought as we parted company at the end of the evening. The following morning John Orgill picked me up as usual, but halfway along the old A38 we found the road flooded. John tried a detour through Willington and Repton, but the

The scene that greeted John Orgill and me when we tried to reach Burton on the morning of 10 December 1965. (Author's Collection)

road was also impassable there, where the River Trent had burst its banks. We tried the other side of the A38, and although Etwall and Egginton were also badly flooded, we eventually managed to get through. Then we discovered that it was the same picture in Derby, where the Derwent was in flood and whole tracts of Darley Abbey, Mansfield Road and Alfreton Road were under water. Fire brigade and police were rescuing residents by boat. It was a remarkable scene. A couple of weeks later, on Boxing Day, Pat and I walked down there to look at the damage. The waters had receded but the stench was terrible; we felt desperately sorry for the people whose homes had been ruined. In the meantime, I'd asked John for a rebate on the bus fare, seeing as he got me into work late that morning, but there was nothing doing, although he did see the funny side. It wasn't the last time the weather closed in when I was at Burton. One Friday afternoon in February 1969 it snowed so heavily that the Blue Bus on which I was travelling home that evening got stuck in Doles Lane and I walked the five miles from Findern back to our house in Young Street, Derby, through huge snowdrifts. At one point traffic was at a standstill in one long line from Littleover back to Lichfield.

Someone else who was always ready for a good laugh was Neville Taylor, a freelance rugby reporter who worked for the Nuneaton Timber Company in the week and covered Burton RFC for us on Saturdays. Neville, who hailed from Dublin, had been a very good rugby player himself, representing All Ireland against the Combined Services during the Second World War. A great joker, he also used to work for the *Burton Mail*, until he himself fell foul of some rugby humour. He'd been told to cover a Burton match in London, but instead was desperate to see Ireland play England at Twickenham on the same day. One of the Burton reserves, a schoolteacher, offered to cover the match for Neville while he slipped off to Twickers. Unfortunately, Burton's game was called off owing to a frost-bound pitch, but in the bar at lunchtime it was decided to send a match report anyway and that afternoon the *Burton Mail* duly published a detailed account of the town team's epic victory in London. Neville might still have got away with it (he returned from Twickenham blissfully unaware that the Burton game had been cancelled) had the *Mail* chairman, Sir Clifford Gothard, not been attending a Rotary Club luncheon two days later. It was too much for a couple of rugby-playing solicitors who had been in on the joke. Sir Clifford had his leg pulled unmercifully, was not at all amused – and that was the end of Neville's reporting career for the paper. He was certainly a character and an evening in his company for a match against a Polish club, who were sponsored by a vodka company and therefore had a coachload of the stuff, is only a very distant memory. One Saturday morning, Neville arrived with a boomerang and we spent an hour on the Ox Hay behind the Market Place, trying to make it come back to us. We were by the Trent Bridge, well on the way out of Burton, before we realised that it would have been a better idea to throw it back and forth, rather than in the same direction every time.

There was also a procession of junior reporters from Derby, sent to Burton to further their skills. One was Mark Sharman, who lived in Jackson Avenue, Mickleover, and who I quickly enlisted into the ranks of

Redfern Athletic. When he was first posted to Burton, Mark joined me on the bus journey into the office each morning until he bought his first car, a battered old Ford Anglia. That summer I booked a family holiday for myself, Pat and our two-year-old daughter, Nicola, at a chalet in the Norfolk seaside resort of Hunstanton. Then I discovered that the railway station there had been closed down. 'No problem', said Mark, 'I'll take you in the car.' Accompanied by Mark's girlfriend, a lovely young lass called Pam, we enjoyed an uneventful journey. Mark and Pam stayed long enough for a sandwich and a cup of tea and then, a week later, came to collect us. Cases piled in the boot, Pam, Pat and Nicola safely squashed on to the back seat, I climbed in next to Mark and tried to close the passenger door which didn't seem all that well aligned. 'It needs a quick jerk up, then a sharp tug towards you', advised our chauffeur. I followed his instructions – and the handle came off in my hand. We scrounged some string from the site manager and eventually set off with me trying to hold the door shut although an occasional slipstream would start to tug it open again. It was an interesting 110-mile journey back to Derby. Mark left the *Telegraph* to work on the *Birmingham Mail* and, a couple of years later, we were shocked to hear that Pam, a young girl so full of life, had died. Mark eventually became managing director of ITV sport. I often wonder if, when he was bossing around the likes of Gabby Logan, he ever chuckled about those days when we heated up Vesta beef curries on a one-ring gas burner, and limped home from Norfolk in his clapped-out jalopy.

Mark Wheeldon was another Burton-based reporter who became a good pal and, just as my two years working at Derby Midland station had introduced me to some colourful people, now I was getting to know a new cast of characters, not least those who worked in the *Telegraph*'s transport department. The department was run by Reg Warner, who was against any form of 'featherbedding' his staff, as he called it. Reg had all the heaters removed from the delivery vans in case the drivers 'get too comfortable and fall asleep'. Neither were the vehicles equipped with windscreen washers. I often scrounged a lift to places like Albert Village and Overseal, in the heart of the South Derbyshire

David Stacey, our bearded chief reporter, and a youngster called Mark Sharman, pictured in the reporters' room at Burton. Mark went on to become one of the most powerful men in television sport. (Author's Collection)

Coalfield, when the job took me there, and it was a nerve-racking experience to be perched beside the driver (there was no passenger seat and, obviously, no seat belt) as he leant out to squirt water from a Fairy Liquid bottle in an attempt to remove coal dust from the windscreen of a delivery van travelling at 40mph. The newspaper wasn't doing anything illegal: in the mid-1960s, road traffic regulations didn't regard things like passenger seats and windscreen washers as essential. The *Telegraph*'s garage in Bourne Street, off Osmaston Road, was also something to behold: the single petrol pump wasn't connected to mains electricity; instead, the drivers had to pump the fuel out by hand. The atmosphere in there was always entertaining, however, and it was a good idea to call in first thing in the morning as each day began with a rather long tea-break.

The drivers were, by and large, a pleasant bunch and I enjoyed listening to their stories: Tommy Hatton was landed on the Normandy coast a full twenty-four hours before D-Day, to help prepare for the Allied invasion of Europe; Les Rhodes had spent two years in North Africa, driving ammunition trucks along 'Messerschmitt Alley'; Jim Blackshaw and Tommy Skinner also had plenty of good war stories to tell and Gordon Longdon was good company on a long journey. One of my favourite characters, though, was Arthur Hawksworth, who had served as a Bevin Boy down the pit. Arthur, who resembled a tall Arthur Askey and whose slightly high-pitched voice had earned him the nickname of Squeak, had a fund of home-spun homilies, chief among which was 'A man who works for nothing and a woman who makes love for nothing are never out of a job.' A strange cove was Tony Richardson, who claimed that he and his wife, although living in the same house, had become estranged to the point where they each used their own frying pan.

Oliver Smith was a familiar figure around Derby. Oliver, who was effectively the deputy circulation manager, was very camp. He had a highly effeminate manner and always wore a cameo brooch on his sports coat lapel. A tall, well-built man, he had a habit of peering at people over half-moon spectacles and it was difficult to ignore him. Not that you would particularly want to; Oliver was a gentlemen. He was also an avid collector of antiques. There was an antiques shop opposite our office in Abbey Arcade and we often received a Monday morning telephone call from Oliver, who'd caught the bus to Burton on the Sunday for a spot of window shopping, asking one of us to nip across the Arcade to ask the price of a snuff box or a brooch. When he died, he was found to own one of the finest collections of ladies' fans in the country. For many years, Oliver lived out in the wilds at Hollington. Each evening he'd get off the bus, pick his bicycle out of the hedgerow where he'd left it that morning, then cycle home for his tea.

There was a weekly visit from Ken Hunt, who came from Derby to sell display advertisements. Ken had two regular clients upon whom he could always count, one of which was a small wool shop. Their business alone seemed to satisfy Ken's bosses, and so he would call in to rubber stamp the orders on his way into the office, stop for a yarn and a pint, and then nip off back to Derby to mow the lawn at his Raven Street home. Advertising revenue was abundant and no-one seemed to worry about targets. Indeed, potential advertisers sometimes had to go on a waiting list because the paper was so full. Occasionally, a man called Harry Robson would come over from Derby to service our teleprinter. Like Dave Stacey, Harry rode a large motor bike. One day we found him scooping up the office collection of pin-up books (nothing offensive in those days, just bikini-clad girls with perhaps the occasional topless model). When Dave challenged him, Harry said that it could be an uncomfortably cold journey travelling up the old A38 on a motor-bike; he needed the magazines as insulation on the trip back to head office. I don't think Dave had the heart to point out that it was the middle of August. Harry's former apprentice, Dave Hannah, was now working at the *Burton Mail* and we became close friends with Dave also dropping into our office to eat his lunchtime sandwiches in a change of scenery.

By and large, not much happened in Burton. Not until the Great Burton Body Mystery, which, over thirty-five years later, has not been solved. One Saturday morning in March 1971 I looked up from my paper on the top deck of a bus going along Newton Road into Burton and saw a white tent pitched just off the road, with police swarming all over the place. The previous evening, a special constable out shooting pigeons had come across the badly decomposed body of a man buried in a sitting position, in a 4ft-deep grave. The body was naked except for a pair of mustard coloured socks and a wedding ring. Most chillingly, his hands were tied behind his back and his feet were also tied together. It was the biggest story our little office had dealt with for years. The police moved mountains in their attempts to identify the man, at one point sending bone and tissue samples to the Smithsonian Institute in Washington where American scientists fixed the victim's age at twenty-nine and determined that he'd been buried for between nine and twelve months. The wedding ring was traced to West Bromwich, but there the trail went cold. Local enquiries revealed no missing person whose description even remotely fitted that of the dead man.

Then the police had what should have been an exciting breakthrough. Experts at Guy's Hospital in London used the skull to recreate the man's features and revealed that, less than six months before his death, he'd undergone expensive and unusual dental treatment. Dentists and dental technicians throughout Britain and abroad were contacted but again the police drew a blank. Hundreds of missing persons files – from a Penzance lighthouse keeper to a Watford milkman, from a gravedigger from the north of England to a man lodging in Ilkeston who had suddenly disappeared – were checked. Each time the answer was negative. There were plenty of rumours, of course, from the story that the man was the victim of a gangland killing to the view that he was a ritual black magic sacrifice, or the result of a sexual deviation that went horribly wrong. The only certain thing was that no-one can tie their hands behind their back, commit suicide and then cover themselves in 4ft of ash. Police certainly believed that the killer had local knowledge. Although the spinney was only a few yards from the relatively busy Newton Road, it was rarely visited by the public. In 2005, I interviewed the special policeman who found the body. David Nathan had no ideas, but he did discount the theory that the victim was an itinerant worker with no fixed abode and probably no National Insurance records. He told me, 'It's an obvious possibility, but for that expensive dental treatment. A drifter would hardly have undergone that just a few months earlier.' In 2006, forensic experts used a computer to create an image of what the man's face may have looked like but, at the time of writing, the mystery remains.

Whatever the truth of the matter, at the time it provided great excitement in our office and was a story that, for once, allowed our edition to keep pace with the *Burton Mail*. The *Mail* was the town's major newspaper, against which the *Telegraph* could normally never hope to compete on an equal footing. Printing on site, the *Mail* could publish local news items almost instantly, whereas the same stories would sometimes take two or three days to appear in the Burton edition of the Derby paper. One problem was that the ancient presses at Northcliffe House were always breaking down. By the time I left the *Telegraph*, it was not uncommon for the first copies of our edition to arrive in Burton as late as 5 p.m. When I started in 1965, we had to work late on Budget days to ensure that news on the price of beer, cigarettes and petrol was carried in the stop press; extra sales were expected on Derby and Grand National days; and big news events like the Aberfan disaster, the first men on the Moon, Southern Rhodesia unilaterally declaring independence, and the escape from prison of Great Train Robber Ronnie Biggs, all involved frantic activity in our little office. A decade later, the role of local newspapers was beginning to change radically, although it would take some time for them to realise it. As for me, one day in April 1975 I was ripping the result of the 2.30 at Redcar from the teleprinter when I realised that I'd probably been doing exactly the same thing in April 1965. That afternoon I saw an advertisement for an assistant manager at the newly opened Derby Sports Centre. On a whim I applied. A week later I attended an interview, at the end of which I was told that I had the job. I was off on another adventure and it would be three years before I returned to the newspaper world which I left it with a great deal of sadness. I'd enjoyed my days at Burton which, in 1965, was still quite an insular town, its traffic continually interrupted by the closing of railway level-crossing gates as grain, hops, malt and then the finished product, beer, were moved back and forth to the Bass, Ind Coope and Marston's breweries that dominated life there. The air hung heavy with the smell of brewing, and practically every family had someone who worked in the industry; sometimes whole generations were employed by the big three brewers. By and large, I found Burtonians an unusual crowd, far less sophisticated than even Derbeians. Our office cleaner had hardly ever left the town; she had certainly never seen the sea, for instance. And she was fairly typical. One of our newspaper sellers, Wally Bridge, was married in Burton but spent his honeymoon in Derby – for the afternoon. After the reception, Wally and his bride, Molly, hopped on a Trent bus and spent the rest of the day travelling down the A38 before returning home; that was a big enough adventure for them. Wally was a strange figure. Thin as a lathe, he had enormous ears (the tops of which he would tuck into his earholes and then flip out again as a party trick) and no teeth. When he wasn't selling papers he worked as a night porter at the Newton Park

Hotel. In 1971, when John Orgill married Lucy, they spent their wedding night at the Newton Park. The following morning they were awakened by the *Evening Telegraph*'s star newspaper seller looming over them carrying a tray of tea. 'I thought I was having a nightmare', said John later.

While John was having recurring bad dreams, Mark Wheeldon and I enrolled in the George Street club where we played snooker most lunchtimes. Some days I would join Dave Stacey for a pleasant stroll across the Ox Hay, and over the Ferry Bridge to Stapenhill and a pint in the Punch Bowl. There wasn't really much else to do. Burton had very few major retail outlets in the 1960s. The market was a hive of activity on Thursdays and Saturdays, but strolling around the shops meant nothing more than a trip through Woolworths or Marks & Spencer. If we weren't heating up our food in the tiny kitchen at Abbey Arcade, or enjoying a pint and a sandwich in the Royal Oak, we'd occasionally have a plate of liver and onions at Eaton's café in New Street, or fish and chips at Tommy's Fish Bar opposite. We did, however, withdraw our patronage from the Dog and Partridge on the High Street after I went into the kitchen one lunchtime to find someone who could take our money, only to discover a large ginger cat snoring away happily in the middle of a tray of pork chops.

Give or take the odd worry over food poisoning Burton provided a gentle existence, although being sited on the Market Place had its disadvantages: every Thursday and Saturday for ten years the peace outside our window was shattered by the owner of a fruit stall yelling, 'Apples a pound pears!' every couple of minutes. That, though, was as nothing compared to the annual statutes fair each September when we had to contend with a cakewalk and its generator shaking the wall for three whole days. Yet if noisy greengrocers and vibrating fairground rides occasionally interrupted us, we remained largely untroubled by head office. Every now and again one of us would have to field calls from Norman Peace, the news editor back in Derby, when he was looking for Dave. 'I can't understand it', he said late one afternoon. 'Do you have staggered lunchtimes there?' I was thinking about saying something witty about, yes, staggering back from the pub, but thought better of it. Norman always sounded like a man who had never even heard of a sense of humour, although his bark was probably worse than his bite. He certainly never visited the office, nor did anyone else in authority. We were left to our own devices. As long as a constant flow of news stories (mostly mundane court cases, inquests and council meetings) were submitted, copies of the papers distributed efficiently, and the local newsagents paid their bills on time, no one bothered us.

Looking back, it was almost idyllic, not least because for most of my time there I travelled back and forth each day with the Blue Bus Company of Tailby and George whose double-deckers rolled along the quiet country roads of South Derbyshire, through the pleasant villages of Findern, Willington, Repton and on to Newton Solney, where the washlands of the River Trent spread out below. Occasionally, I'd catch their other service that meandered through Etwall, Egginton, Hilton and Stretton. Either way, it was a world far removed from W.H. Smith's and those bitterly cold and foggy days spent on lonely railway platforms, wondering if the train home to Derby would ever turn up.

CHAPTER THIRTEEN

Drink Your Beers, My Little Dears

It must have been someone's stag night. We'd just crowded into the Mousetrap bar of the Cheshire Cheese on St Peter's Street and our kittymaster, John Cheadle, said to the barmaid, 'Twenty-three pints of bitter, please.' She looked down her nose: 'Sorry, we don't serve pints in this bar.' Undaunted, Cheadle replied, 'Well all right then, give us forty-six halves.' Of course, she was having none of it and we were soon on our way again. That was the drinking scene in Derby in the early 1960s. Pubs were for mature adults, not for cocky youths who were only just old enough to drink legally. Unlike today, when city-centre drinking is targeted at the young, over forty years ago late teenage youths had to serve what almost amounted to an apprenticeship before they were accepted into pubs which were usually the preserve of white male adults of middle age or older. Even after we had turned eighteen, it was more likely that we'd spend the evening in a coffee bar than in a pub.

The more sophisticated of Derby's young men and women went to the Boccaccio coffee bar in the Market Place, one of those trendy 'Italian' places that sprang up all over Britain in the early 1960s. Around the corner there was the Kardomah which tended to cater for business people and for families. For us, however, it was the Genevieve coffee house in

A quiet drink in the Duke of York in the 1960s. Left to right are Derek Grantham, Sid Sharp, Alan Dobson and Dave Keeling. (Author's Collection)

Gower Street because the owner, Sid Greatorex, offered us such a warm welcome. Sid, a tailor by trade, ran the newly opened Genevieve with his wife, although in due course, they parted and he married a younger girl who had been one of their waitresses. Sid, who walked with a pronounced limp, was a bit of a character whose catchphrase was, 'No rules, no regulations here', although there were actually plenty of house rules to keep customers in check. Not that they were needed: the youth of forty-odd years ago seemed happy enough to spend their evenings in pleasant conversation; looking for a fight didn't come into it. In the early 1960s, Sid's coffee house became our unofficial headquarters, the place where we held our football club meetings, celebrated birthdays, laughed and joked until he kicked us out at 10 p.m. One Friday evening there was great excitement when the Chelsea football team arrived. They were playing in Sheffield and were stopping in Derby overnight. This was the Swinging Sixties, the King's Road and all that, and Chelsea footballers epitomised the era. Terry Venables and his pals were happy enough to sit drinking coffee in public, chatting to other customers and signing autographs. It's hard to imagine Frank Lampard and Co. mixing like that today.

When a bowling alley opened in Colyear Street – like coffee houses, ten-pin bowling was a trend that spread through Britain like wildfire in the mid-1960s – some of our number switched their patronage, while evenings spent at the Genevieve became fewer. I was never a regular patron of the bowling alley, instead finding myself drinking in the Queen's Hotel in Crompton Street where my boyhood pal, Stuart Clay (who lived opposite the pub), was a regular. The landlord, Ted Taylor, was a nice enough chap who always announced closing time with a sing-song, 'Drink your beers my little dears; it's the only time the law's on my side.' Ted was helped behind the bar by his wife, daughter and son-in-law, and they were a pleasant family who created the perfect atmosphere for a little back-street boozer. One night, however, I witnessed a scene that made me cringe, one which gets no easier to contemplate with the passage of time. Pat and I were sitting in the lounge when a couple came in. The man was West Indian, the woman was white. It wasn't exactly a rarity to see two people of different races together, but it wasn't all that usual either. Mixed marriages were still frowned upon and the offspring of such relationships often had a hard time. Seeing that someone else had served them, Ted was round from the bar in a flash. The couple were sitting at the next table to us and he told them to leave, or at least to move into the bar. The worst aspect of all of this was the resigned look on the black man's face. He accepted the ruling without question and they picked up their drinks and shuffled back through to the bar to finish them before, a few moments later, leaving. I felt terribly uncomfortable at the time and, in retrospect, always wish that we'd also got up and left in protest. These were different times, of course, and Ted Taylor was a nice man in all other respects, but the thought of the indignity he heaped upon the couple that evening has stayed with me ever since.

Shortly after that episode, we did transfer our custom, from the Queen's to the White Horse in the Morledge. The White Horse was run by Alice Baker, a matriarchal figure whose brother was the famous Derby racing driver, Reg Parnell. Alice's husband, who was always known as 'the Old Scholar', had died and the real running of the pub was in the hands of Charles Boneham, an unmarried, slightly camp figure. While Charles served behind the bar, Alice would hold court with her pals in 'the Virgin's Corner'. Occasionally she would make a move, usually to see if any young couple was holding hands. Alice disapproved of physical contact between people of the opposite sex and would soon pre-empt any hanky-panky with a curt, 'Now then, none of that in here!' Heaven knows what she would have made of today's permissive society; an evening of twenty-first-century television viewing, even before the watershed, would probably have finished her off. Charles allowed us to run the Redfern Athletic tote at the White Horse, which, of course, brought him a bigger clientele on a Sunday evening when the tote was drawn. Unlike today, few pubs sold food – a bag of crisps or a pickled egg if you were lucky – but Charles was always proud of his sandwiches and cobs. One Sunday lunchtime we were enjoying a pint in the White Horse when a woman in her sixties, face heavily made up, came in and ordered a bottle of milk stout. Then she pointed to the food cabinet on the bar and said in a rather snotty voice, 'Barman, are these sandwiches fresh?' I thought Charles was going to explode. Instead, he adjusted his spectacle and snorted, 'Madam, the only thing fresher than those sandwiches is me.' I laughed so much that beer came down my nose. Sadly, when Alice died, Charles quickly found himself out of a job and a home.

Although the White Horse was our main drinking venue in 1960s Derby, that wasn't to say that we didn't become acquainted with quite a few of the town's other hostelries, some of them quite unsavoury. Drinking in them just amused us. The Globe in Irongate had a particularly dodgy reputation. Today it is called Mr Jorrocks and is famous as part of the George coaching inn where some of Bonnie Prince Charlie's rebel rag-tag army stayed in December 1745. We used to sit in the Globe just to watch the 'ladies of easy virtue' disappear round the back with an off-duty railway porter or postman before returning a few minutes later to continue sipping the glass of Mackeson stout they'd left half-drunk at the bar. Across the road from the Globe, the Wine Vaults in the Market Place was another of Derby's town-centre pubs with a bad reputation. It was known locally as 'the Sough', a word that meant a drain; that just about summed up the nightly goings-on there. Yet John Cheadle managed to get us barred from the place, which was no mean achievement considering the low life that frequented it. Again, it must have been someone's stag night – it wasn't the sort of place you'd ordinarily patronise – and one of our crowd accidentally broke a glass. The landlord demanded payment for it, but John argued that it was an accident and, in any case, we'd just bought a round for about twenty people. It may have been John saying 'Now look here, my good man . . . ' that particularly annoyed mine host but he erupted and threw us all out, for good measure banning us from ever again entering his premises (which was unlikely anyway). There was the undignified sight of people furiously gulping down the ale they'd just bought before being ejected from the pub. A few years later, the council demolished the Wine Vaults to make way for Derby's new Assembly Rooms. Few mourned its passing.

Our little crowd achieved what many thought was impossible – being banned from the Wine Vaults, pictured here next door to Barlow & Taylor's store. Scaffolding encases the old Assembly Rooms after it was badly damaged by fire in 1963. (Derby Evening Telegraph)

These were the venues where Derby's low life hung out, although the criminal underclass were largely invisible to anyone but the police. There were also very few drunks. An Irish labourer named John McCormick achieved notoriety by being banned from every pub and off-licence in the town. Yet his name still appeared regularly in the *Evening Telegraph* when he made yet another court appearance for being drunk and disorderly. The number of his convictions ran well into three figures. About the only other celebrated drunks were Winnie and Ronnie Bradbury, and their friend, Lil Elliott. The trio could usually be found sitting on the window sill of the post office in Victoria Street, swigging from bottles of cider. Ronnie had been a sailor in his younger days. His face was sunburnt, almost the colour of a chestnut, and his nose was flattened against his face, the result of bar-room brawls on several continents. Winnie, who also went by the name of Winnie Austin, and Lil had at one time worked as prostitutes, or so rumour had it, although it was hard to imagine that they ever drummed up many clients. Yet this unholy trinity, even when they were roaring drunk, really didn't pose a threat to anyone, certainly not to passers-by. Their occasional court appearances usually came after they'd caused trouble in the Labour Exchange on Normanton Road. In later years, the lower end of Normanton Road, running into Rosehill Street, became infamous as Derby's red light area, which was sad for the decent residents of all colours who eventually found themselves marooned there as the nature of the neighbourhood changed dramatically. In the 1950s and early 1960s, however, it was the Meadows, between Nottingham Road and the Derwent, that had that unsavoury reputation. It was an area into which few people would venture, one of those almost mythical places that belong to local folklore. There was one character of whom everyone had heard: Cattle Market Kate. In fact, I believe she was simply a generic figure, a composite of all the ladies of the night who plied their trade down there.

The centre of Derby was certainly a safe place to drink at night, although one Saturday lunchtime in the early 1970s I had an unpleasant experience at The Bell Hotel. Pat had asked me to nip into town to buy something and, task completed, I fancied a beer before returning home. I was halfway down my pint when a large man with a shock of red hair, who had been leaning on the other end of the Dilly Bar, came over, gulped down the rest of my drink – and then began to eat the glass. There he was, biting off chunks of glass and chewing them, blood streaming from his lips; and there I was, wondering whether to say anything, or just buy him another empty glass to be sociable. Fortunately, the landlord wandered in from one of the other bars and saw what was happening. His reaction was unusual and inventive: he told my new drinking chum that he was barred – for not wearing a tie. Neither was I, so I quietly slipped off my seat and disappeared into Sadler Gate without waiting for the outcome.

Another character of note was a great shambling man universally known as Pigeon Percy because of his habit of feeding pigeons. Percy was never a threat to anyone; he just shuffled along all day with a nub end quivering on his bottom lip. He was a familiar figure in the town centre, almost part of the street furniture, but I never heard him speak one word. However, my friend Stan Tacey, who worked at Bemrose's printers and was, for many years, scorer to Derbyshire County Cricket Club, told the story of how Percy was sitting on his own front doorstep one fine summer's day, watching workmen file back into a nearby factory after their dinner break. 'Look at that silly lot', he told Stan, 'and they reckon I'm barmy.' Percy would often keep Florrie Birtles company. Florrie was an *Evening Telegraph* newspaper seller whose pitch was the steps of the Boots building on the corner of St Peter's Street and East Street. There were no little red boxes to protect sellers from the worst of Derby's weather so Florrie was often absent, having nipped across the road to the Green Man in St Peter's Churchyard, leaving the morose Percy to oversee a kind of honour system whereby people were supposed to leave the few coppers for their newspaper inside her paperbag. Come to think of it, Florrie was just as likely to be in the pub on a warm summer's day, so the weather probably didn't have much to do with it.

Sometimes we'd stroll up to the top of Irongate to the Irongate Hotel, which had originally been built as offices and a bottling facility for a firm of vintners called Cox & Bowring. It became an hotel and bar sometime in the 1920s and, when we patronised it in the early 1960s, it was still run on a six-day licence, closing on Sundays. It was a dour place, as most hotel bars were in those days, the only highlight being the little white-haired waitress called Gladys who brought our drinks across and who always accepted the offer of 'a thrill', which was a shilling's worth of sherry. In 1968, the Irongates Hotel became a Berni Inn (it had already converted itself into what nowadays would be known as a 'fun pub' by

Irongate in the late 1950s. The Irongate Hotel (left) sold the local Offilers' brew. (Author's Collection)

adding a German-style cellar bar) and has since undergone several changes of identity. A hotel bar that was always packed was that of the St James's Hotel in (funnily enough) St James's Street. In the 1960s, Jimmy's, like all town-centre pubs, catered for a middle-aged, or older, market. Couples who fancied a night out in town, away from their own neighbourhood, would travel in on Corporation petrol or trolley buses, enjoy a few drinks – usually pints of bitter or mild for the man, port and lemon for the woman – and then do the reverse journey without any fear of being mugged on the way home, even on the darkest night. Any youngsters even talking too loudly (in the opinion of older pub-goers) would soon be put in their place.

That isn't to say that there weren't the occasional incidents outside a pub, even at the Marquis of Granby in Gerard Street. On more than one occasion on a Saturday night, I lay in bed listening to a fight going on down the street at chucking-out time. The difference was that such scraps were fought almost under Queensberry Rules; just fists, no feet. And quite definitely no knives. Undoubtedly the most spectacular fight I ever saw outside a pub, however, was at the Melbourne Arms on Normanton Road one Saturday night when a drunken Irishman was taking on half a dozen policemen who were trying to get him into the back of a Black Maria. Police helmets littered the pavement as they battled with him. Eventually they pinned him to the ground, one of them sitting on his chest. Suddenly, he gave an almighty roar and rose up, the officer on his chest being catapulted into the air. Then the whole battle started again. After a while I got bored and continued on my way. I wondered if it was

John McCormick, the Irishman banned from every pub in Derby, but the following Monday's *Evening Telegraph* carried no report of the incident, so I will never know if I saw the legend in action that night.

Derby's clubs weren't that much more exciting than the pubs. We joined Rick Moylan's Windmill Club, next door to the Corporation Hotel on the edge of the Cattle Market, just to get a late drink on a Thursday night. For the same reason we also became members of the Curzon Club in Colyear Street. The Windmill just offered drinks and a buffet (tiny curled-up sandwiches and something called Kunzle cakes, named after a Swiss chef who used to work at the House of Commons), together with the promise of a striptease act that today would probably be considered extremely tame. The Curzon, though, was a bit more upmarket and also had gambling – poker, blackjack and roulette – although I never had enough money to waste on such pursuits. While I lived in Gerard Street, home was only a ten-minute walk from the town centre, whereas the other lads, all of whom lived in the suburbs, had to make sure they were in Victoria Street before the Corporation bus inspector blew his whistle and the last buses pulled away. Otherwise it was a long walk because taxis were hard to find in Derby's town centre in the 1960s.

Eventually, of course, the responsibilities of married life and fatherhood overtook most of us. By the middle of the 1970s, our nights out in Derby had drawn to a close. It was the end of an era. The pubs were changing and so was their clientele. Thirty years later, we'd feel like visitors from another planet.

CHAPTER FOURTEEN

Ghosts

On a baking summer's day in 2006, I found myself outside our old house in Gerard Street, looking up to where Ramsden's bakery had once shared the end of Webster Street with the Premier Pattern Company. The house where I was born was one of the few remaining in Gerard Street. Most of the others had been demolished, replaced by one-storey homes dotted around where people had once sat in their back yards on such a day. Webster Street, however, looked much the same and on this journey of rediscovery I wandered to the top to look at John Burns's old house. Number 16 appeared unchanged since the days we listened to the overture to the *Pirates of Penzance* on the Burnses' old wind-up gramophone. I thought about going down the entry, to stand where we pinged air-rifle pellets off the roofs in Rosengrave Street, but thought better of it in case the man who threatened to clip us round the ear was, by some remote chance, still alive and, by an even greater chance, still sprightly enough to carry out his threat.

Instead, I retraced my steps until I was on the corner once more, wondering which way to go. Two young lads, both of whom should probably have been at school, came wandering across. 'All right, mate?' one of them asked. I explained that, long ago, when dinosaurs roamed the earth, I'd played in these same streets. The concept of nostalgia understandably eluded them and they sidled off towards town, probably on their way to buy some solvent, I thought uncharitably. Suddenly, my mind drifted back to a scene, fifty years earlier. It is the start of the school holidays and all us kids have gathered to decide what to do with the ocean of a day that lies ahead of us. Someone suggests Darley Park. Someone else, Normanton Park. In the end someone produces a cricket bat and we stay where we are. Street cricket is safe because Webster Street is a cul-de-sac and the only traffic is going to be from the occasional delivery van, laden with freshly baked bread and cakes, leaving Ramsden's. There are local rules: if the ball is hit over our long garden wall, the batsman (or batswoman) will score 'six and out'; and, to avoid fruitless arguments, we have dispensed with the leg-before-wicket law. I don't even have to close my eyes to hear the voices of my childhood.

'That was out', insists Colin Shaw.

'No', says John Burns, 'it missed the wicket.'

'There's chalk on the ball', cries Colin, triumphantly holding aloft a battered tennis ball on which there may, or may not, be a faint white smudge.

The dispute is settled in time-honoured fashion: three bat handles. John has to face the next three deliveries while holding his bat upside down; if he survives, he can stay.

That afternoon, household chores out of the way, our mothers will gather on doorsteps to natter. My own mother will probably find an excuse to visit Violet Craven's little shop on the opposite corner of Webster Street, not to buy anything but to gossip. It is what people did before counselling was invented. Back in July 2006, Violet's shop had long gone, replaced by council flats. The bakery and the print works that replaced it had also closed, the site now the subject of a controversial plan to build yet more flats. The street was now dotted with cars (none of these houses was ever built with a garage) so, even if I'd felt up to sending down a few more overs against the imaginary chalked wicket on the wall of our old house, it would have been impossible. Black wheelie bins also posed a threat to a good-length ball. Most residents took their bins, once emptied, round the back. A few, though, apparently couldn't be bothered. Time moves on, and with it attitudes change; some might say that standards fall, but the purpose of my visits wasn't to make moral judgements. Suddenly I was aware that the two boys had returned and, from the other side of Webster Street, were viewing me with some suspicion. I decided that it was time to move on before someone made a telephone call about a strange man hanging around talking to kids and I finished up at the new police station on what had once been St Mary's Wharf, trying to explain this nostalgia business to a burly sergeant who wasn't from the *Dixon of Dock Green* school of coppering. Trying to look more purposeful, I walked off towards where Grey Street and Harcourt Street formed a crossroads with Gerard Street. I tried to work out where Colin Shaw's house once stood, and maybe got to within a house either way. Colin had told me that he could identify it from an old drain cover; or was it a lamp-post?

Then I tried to line up Kathleen Radford's, and from there the big house where first Mrs Watkins and then Steve Parboo rented out rooms, their combined efforts spanning the dying days of one era and the birth pangs of another. At the corner of Grey Street, it was easy to locate where the grocer's shop had once stood and where Sylvia's husband had paid me a penny a go to say a swear word in a posh accent. For years after the coronation of 1953 you could still see crosses painted on the pavements in Grey Street to indicate where tubs of flowers were placed when the residents won a competition for the best decorated street in Derby. Now a million raindrops, and maybe as many footsteps, had erased the markers from all but memory. Grey Street's old houses had also gone, again replaced by council flats. I wondered whatever became of Mrs Theobold, a fierce looking white-haired woman with a face so red that it looked as if she scrubbed it every morning with a stiff brush and bar of carbolic soap. And Johnny Powell, who was in the same class as me at Becket School and whose nose ran perpetually, an affliction which earned him an unflattering nickname. It was a memory which still made me shudder. I moved on.

At the bottom of Grey Street it was hard to believe that the postage stamp of land at the corner of Spa Lane and Abbey Street had once been home to the Lord Belper; it must have been very cramped on Saturday nights. After they knocked the pub down, the council had erected a small fence around the little patch of ground and planted some bushes; now the fence guarded only bare earth. Small industrial units sat where people had once gathered by their firesides in small front rooms, or queued in Abbey Street's shops. A light industrial firm now occupied the place where Donald Sims had been arbitrarily certified insane by my mother. A few doors away, where the Co-op cake shop had done a brisk trade, two morose-looking men sat at the entrance to a car wash, waiting for a dirty vehicle or going-home time, whichever came first. For a moment I considered walking up to Boyer Street but then decided to leave the ghost of Tommy Harris for another day. Instead I began a measured stroll towards town, past where Gran Rowley's tobacconist's shop had stood opposite Stockbrook Street, and where Cousin Fred had painted those pictures as he tried to forget the horrors of the First World War. Even though every shop and house had gone, Fred would surely still have recognised the area. Treading in the footsteps of ancestors can be a strange feeling.

Earlier that year I'd found the answer to the question: whatever happened to Cousin Fred? Remarkably, Fred Densham, the man who my family thought was dead, had again survived wartime captivity and was still alive in the 1970s. Jonathan Moffatt, a Coventry man who ran a website for people interested in British Malaya, had plenty of information. After more than twenty years on the Malayan peninsula, Fred was better placed than many to survive the horrors of Changi internment camp. And survive he did. Released in 1945, he returned to planting at Sungei Kahang Estate, Kluang, Johore. Like many British planters, he took a Chinese wife, and he adopted two Chinese daughters. Fred, by now manager of a 5,600-acre plantation, one of the largest out there, retired in 1956, and in December 1969, the year he was made a life member of the Incorporated Society of Planters, was living in retirement back in Penang. He died in May 1972. John Hedley, a retired planter who now lives at Solihull, remembered him well: 'We called him "Soldier" Densham. He was well known throughout the British community in Malaya. He was the doyen of the club, a generous man.' Why did we lose touch with him? Late in 1941, of course, my family moved back to Derby to escape the heavy bombing on Hull. Perhaps when he was released from captivity, Fred wrote to them at the last address he had, but received no reply. Perhaps after three years in a Japanese PoW camp, tracking down relatives in England wasn't such a priority. It is hard to imagine in these days of e-mail and mobile phones, but communicating halfway across the world wasn't always so easy. But at least I know what happened to Cousin Fred.

Moving from Hull may have been partly to blame for us losing touch with Fred, but during my childhood, that city seemed to dominate our daily life. I knew most of the stories off by heart: the narrow escape from the shrapnel; the dogfight over the river when a Spitfire pilot shot down an enemy plane and all the neighbours cheered; the three soldiers killed by a blast bomb that left them outwardly unmarked; the little girl blown into my parents' garden. Hull seemed to have played such an important part in their lives that eventually I'd felt compelled to visit the city.

Standing outside the house in Aisne Street, Hull, some sixty years after my parents left there after the houses opposite were destroyed by the Luftwaffe.

Pulling into Paragon railway station, the sense that I was walking in their footsteps was overwhelming. I recalled the time when my mother had arrived back after a visit to Derby, just as the air-raid warning sirens wailed out and everyone was made to remain on the train while bombs dropped all around the station. A bus took me to Chanterlands Avenue, which was a familiar name, and from there I walked to Aisne Street. The house was as I'd always imagined it, on the end of a row with the allotments where the anti-aircraft guns had been sited still there. I stood for a few moments, trying to imagine that Sunday morning in September 1939 when they learned that war had been declared. Then I tried to imagine my father walking from the bus stop on his way home from work. Apart from the row of new houses opposite, where the bomb had fallen in 1941, it was a scene he would undoubtedly have recognised. From one of the original houses further down the opposite side of the street, a little woman appeared. 'Can I help you?' she asked. I explained that my parents had lived at no.1 during the war.

'Oh, do you mean Mrs Rippon?' she said. I was shocked. The woman must have been a small child when war broke out. How strange to reach out well over sixty years and touch another, almost mythical, age. To my later regret, I didn't ask her name, or what other memories she had. What did she remember of my parents? It was a question that was to remain unasked.

Back in Gerard Street, I looked again at the wall on which we had chalked our wicket and against which we had kicked our football until dusk. Then it was time to go home for tea.